"Change yourself and change the world."

Anonymous

Your Rebel Life

Rebel Diva Book Three

Hack Your Habits and Boost Your Life

100 Tips to Elevate and Enhance the Ten Pillars of Your Life

Copyright ©2019 Tikiri Herath
Edition: 2019
Library & Archives Canada Cataloging in Publication
ISBN: 978-1-989232-08-8

Author: Tikiri Herath
Publisher: The Rebel Diva Academy®
Proofread and Editing: Stephanie Parent
Copy Editing: Deborah Dove
Cover Design: Angela O e-covers
Formatting: Aelurus Publishing
Author Shot: Aura Mckay

All rights reserved. The use of any part of this publication, reproduced, transmitted in any form or by any means electronic, mechanical, photocopying, recording, or otherwise or stored in a retrieval system without prior written consent of the publisher—or in the case of photocopying or other reprographic copying, a license from the Canadian Copyright Licensing Agency—is an infringement of the copyright law.

Tikiri

The advice and strategies contained here may not be suitable or applicable to everyone or to every situation. Reading this work does not construe an engagement between the author/publisher and the reader, and the author/publisher is not rendering any legal, psychological, accounting or any other professional services through this work. Neither the author nor the publisher will be liable for damages arising from here.

The books and website links cited here are only for information and educational purposes and does not mean the author or the publisher endorses everything provided via these external resources. While the author will make every effort to ensure the links in this book remain updated, there is no guarantee the external sites may always be available or provide what they had initially.

TABLE OF CONTENTS

Rebel Defined	vii
Who This Book Is For	viii
The Rebel Diva Series	ix
The Fire in Your Belly	11
The Heroine's Journey	19
The Passion Pyramid	23
INTRODUCTION	29
SECTION One: Feel Well	61
SECTION Two: Sleep Well	89
SECTION Three: Move Well	113
SECTION Four: Eat Well	139
SECTION Five: Learn Well	167
SECTION Six: Work Well	195
SECTION Seven: Invest Well	225
SECTION Eight: Think Well	253
SECTION Nine: Love Well	277
SECTION Ten: Play Well	301
SECTION Eleven: My Pledge	323
Exclusive Gift	330
Fifty Books List	332
Fifty Virtual Mentors	336
About the Author	342
A Free Story	343

Own Your Life. Be a Rebel Diva.

Rebel

NOUN

plural: rebels

Pronunciation /ˈrɛb(ə)l/

A person who resists authority, control, or convention.

Diva

NOUN

plural: divas

Pronunciation /ˈdēvə/

Goddess. Feminine of divus divine. Late 19th century Italian derived from Latin.

I dedicate this book to *you*.

These books are for you if you long, more than anything, to burst out of your shell into the open and live the life you dream about.

To you I say, never stop dreaming. And never, ever give up the pursuit of your passions.

The Rebel Diva Workbooks

www.RebelDivas.com

Sign up to get your exclusive gift!

This Rebel Diva booklet comes with three essential decision-making tools to help you overcome any anxieties when faced with life's challenges. Click on the cover or go to the link below to get your free copy and also learn about exclusive and free training at the Rebel Diva Academy.

https://www.rebeldivas.com/rebel-life-page/

Your Rebel Life

> *"I wish I were a girl again, half savage and hardy and free...*
> *Why am I so changed? I'm sure I should be myself were I once*
> *among the heather on those hills."*
> *Emily Brontë*

A FIRE IN YOUR BELLY

We all hold a precious dream within us—a fire burning in our belly.

Yes, every one of us.

Some of us hide our dreams because we're too scared to look our truth in the face. Some of us have valiantly tried to bring those dreams out in the open but quickly stashed them away because of what someone said or how someone judged us. Then, there are some of us who ignore our dreams, pretending they don't exist because acknowledging them would mean we'd be compelled to do something.

The result is graveyards full of women who've been buried with their dreams untouched. Imagine what they could have achieved if they'd stood proudly and taken ownership of their future. Imagine what inspiration they'd have given to the next generation of girls, creating a ripple effect that uplifts us all.

THE WORLD IS YOURS

We're all capable, *more* than capable, of bringing our dreams to light.

Yes, that means you.

This world can be yours. The future can be yours. All you need to do is bravely step up, grab life by the horns and ride it. You must take ownership of your future. No one else can do that for you. And there is no better time to start your life's amazing ride than today.

IGNORE THE NAYSAYERS

Why do we wait for a life-changing event like sickness, death, layoff, bankruptcy, separation, or divorce—times when we don't have a choice but to wake up and make drastic changes? Why let others dictate who we are and what we must do?

Most people go through their days in a trance without understanding who they truly are, what they're doing or where they're going.

We, especially women, feel burdened by the expectations others put on us, or many times, by the demands we place on ourselves. Without a clear vision for our lives, we're easily manipulated to meet the interests of others—people who've already figured out what they want in life.

Naysayers can be persistent and hard to ignore, especially if they're family and friends. But if you can summon the courage to stand in your power, you'll get an enormous boost in your energy, vitality, and happiness. This will catapult you to your dream life.

Remember, how others judge us is only a reflection of their own insecurities, fears, and worries, or their need to keep us under their control.

So, stop listening to what they say and start following your dreams right this minute.

SUMMON YOUR COURAGE

Where do we start?

First, find an ounce of courage inside you.

Then, do some soul-searching and look for those aspirations longing to jump out. Protect and nurture those dreams.

Finally, you must act. All the dreaming and wishing and hoping in the world won't make anything come alive. Only pure action will do so.

This doesn't have to be scary or difficult. This can be a fun and fulfilling ride. And you're not alone. We will take this journey together.

These books were designed to take you by the hand on an expedition of self-discovery, goal setting, and habit-forming so you can start living your life—the one you wish to have, not the one others expect of you.

Don't be afraid to stand at the edge of your comfort zone. Feel that tingle of fear mixed with excitement and give it a whirl with plenty of support and cheering from the rest of us. You'll find your sense of self-worth grow and your inner strength surge. You'll wake up every day feeling good about yourself and confident in who you are.

More importantly, your vision will expand and you'll see beyond yourself. And this is where magic happens. When you grow, the lives of those surrounding you will also grow. You'll become an amazing role model for your daughters, your sisters, your neighbors, your colleagues, and more.

This is what will make you a true Rebel Diva. A strong and proud woman who stands in her own power and inspires those around her. You'll become the wonder woman we all look up to.

Now, isn't that a life worth living?

> *"An unexamined life is not worth living."*
> Socrates

MY GOAL

My aim is to shake you out of your complacency and to spur you to uncover the wonderful gifts you have within you. I want to see you burst out with confidence and a dazzling smile on your face that says, *Watch out world, here I come!*

BUT THESE BOOKS AREN'T FOR EVERYONE

I could have easily created a few pop quizzes and slapped on a sexy title like "The One-Minute Passion Finder," and sold a ton of books. But I'd be lying.

I could have filled pages and pages with pointless platitudes to make you feel good about staying stuck where you are and make a handsome profit. But I'd be cheating.

These books don't give you false shortcuts or magic bullets to solve your problems. I call things as they are and don't mince my words.

So, if you don't want to hear hard truths or ask introspective questions, these workbooks aren't for you. If you dislike addressing issues head-on or if you're not a fan of political incorrectness, I urge you not to read further. It will only aggravate you and I'd hate to do that to you.

If, however, you're looking for practical tips that give you results and don't mind language that is to the point, then read on.

LASTING CHANGE

Change requires courage. And courage requires conviction. These books are for the women of this world who yearn to empower themselves and seek that courage to follow their own path and live true to their calling.

But that kind of lasting change doesn't happen overnight. You must do the work and stay consistent as you walk toward your dreams.

If you're prepared to go against everything you've been taught and do the things most won't dare, these books will open new horizons for you. If you are willing to do the work to enhance your inner strength and create a new future, you're in the right place.

In these workbooks, you'll find how to feed the fire burning in your belly. You'll get in touch with your passions. And you'll feel the fear but do it anyway, without worrying about what others think or say.

And that, my dear sisters, is what will make you a true Rebel Diva.

"The most common way people give up their power is by thinking they don't have any."

Alice Walker

Your Rebel Life

"I am a woman with thoughts and questions and shit to say. I say if I'm beautiful. I say if I'm strong. You will not determine my story. I will."
Amy Schumer

THE HEROINE IS YOU. THE JOURNEY IS YOUR LIFE.

THE HEROINE'S JOURNEY

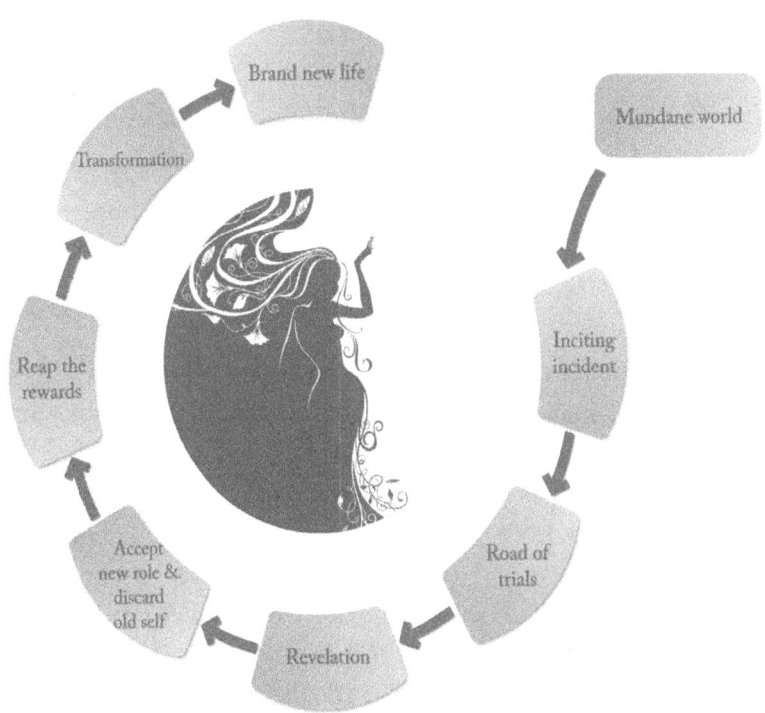

The heroine's journey* is universal. It applies to you whether you are the southern hemisphere or the northern one. It pertains to you regardless of your culture, religion, age, race, sexual orientation or anything else that makes you human.

We all start at stage one—the everyday world—until an incident too arduous for us to handle falls on us, forcing us through this cycle. If we're not ready, the road ahead can be a treacherous one with many troubles along the way.

Some of us may never recover from the inciting incident and succumb to it. Others may get lost, taking wrong turns and feeling every strain of their journey. Then, there will be some of us who will carry on pretending to live in the same ordinary world, though everything has changed. We'll be living an illusion which will cause us to crash and burn even faster than the original event.

We all undergo this cycle in our lives. And for some of us, more than once. It's inevitable. It's what being human is all about.

So, what do we do?

Here are two questions to ask yourself:

- Am I going to sit and wait for life-changing events to trip me up, or can I proactively create the life I deserve starting today?
- Am I going to think of negative incidents as hopeless failures, or can I look at them as calls to adventure—a call to creating a brand-new life?

We're all going to come across times when we feel sorrow, anger, or fear. These emotions may come from something that happened, what someone said, or even a mistake we made that leaves us berating ourselves for days on end. Feeling bad (in its many forms) is normal. It's when we don't face our emotions, run away from them or blame others that problems arise.

We have to learn to acknowledge our feelings. We need to look at what happened dead straight in the eye and decide how we will respond to it. We must take control of how we resolve the difficult things in life. This means pushing our fears and worries away and moving over to the driver's seat to become the navigators of our own futures.

In these pages, you'll find the ideas and concepts that put you in the driver's seat. This doesn't mean you'll be immune to the troubles of life, but you'll get the foresight, the tools, and the knowledge to maneuver your way around them with the least pain and the most gain to you.

Are you ready to become the heroine of your own life?

---

*Based on Joseph Campbell's legendary theory of the twelve-step Hero's Journey.

Your Rebel Life

THE PASSION PYRAMID

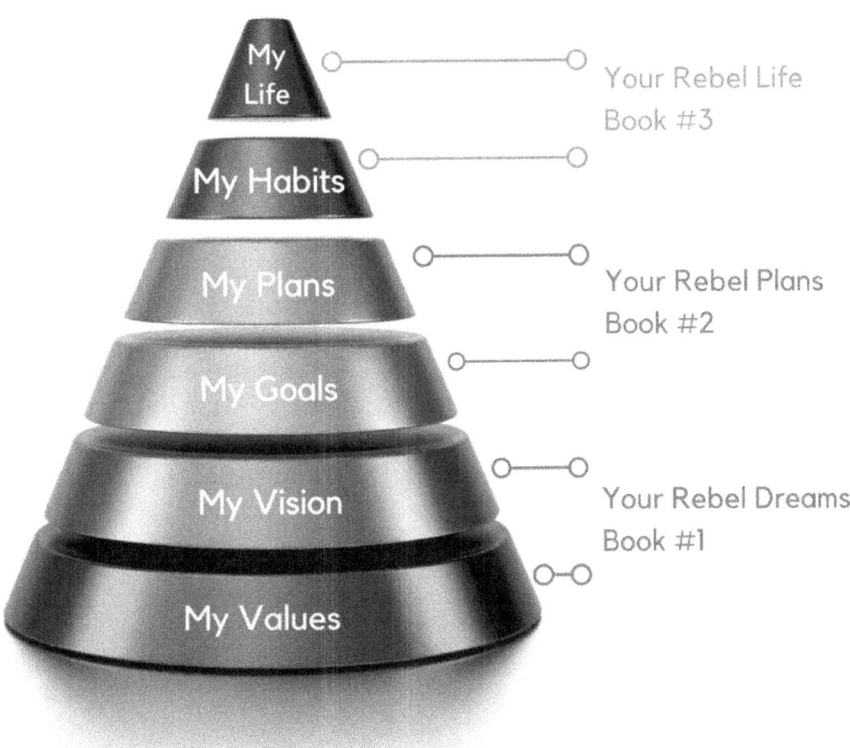

Your Rebel Life

"I am no bird and no net ensnares me. I am a free human being with an independent will."

Jane Eyre

THE PASSION PYRAMID

You'll need a clear vision and a roadmap to take control over your life. You'll also need to embrace the right mindset and good habits to create the life you desire.

The mandate of this Rebel Diva series is to provide you with that knowledge and skill, with easy-to-follow exercises based on the all-encompassing Passion Pyramid.

As the pyramid shows, your personal values form the base for your life vision, your vision determines your goals, and your goals formulate your plans.

Ultimately, your vision, your goals, and your plans are sustained by your daily habits and mindset.

For this to work, you must:

- Be uncompromising on your personal values
- Be resolute in your life vision
- Be intentional, yet savvy, with your goals
- Be focused on but adaptable with your plans
- Be regular and consistent in your habits

THE REBEL DIVA BOOKS

Each of the Rebel Diva books focuses on a couple steps of this pyramid, moving from the base to the top.

The first book—*Your Rebel Dreams*—helps you uncover your *why*, that is, your purpose and your passions, culminating in your *what*, which is your vision.

The second book—*Your Rebel Plans*—shows you how to design a life around your new vision. It captures the stages of goal setting, action planning, and tracking your progress.

The third book—*Your Rebel Life*—helps you create and foster the right habits in the ten most important pillars of your life so you can pursue your aspirations with joy.

THIS BOOK BELONGS TO

Rebel Diva	

Location	

Date	

PRINT EXERCISES IN BOOK

Download the PDF worksheet booklet for *Your Rebel Life*.

This booklet includes worksheets for all the exercises in this book. You can print them, write your answers directly on them, pin them up if you'd like and refer to them every day.

Tap on the link below to download your free private copy.

Your Rebel Life Worksheet Booklet

https://www.rebeldivas.com/rebel-life-page/

INTRODUCTION

LET'S START THIS JOURNEY!

"Be certain that you do not die without having done something wonderful for humanity."

Maya Angelou

"You were designed for accomplishment, engineered for success, and endowed with the seeds of greatness."
Zig Ziglar

SUCCESS

Over the past two decades, I obsessed about finding an answer to what success meant.

After years of observing, I realized a person's status in society is not a translation of true progress, achievement or maturity. Neither are careers, connections or cash.

Success, to me, is measured by how great of a human being an individual has become, and that greatness comes from cultivating a character of substance. That, in essence, defines a successful person.

So, what is a character of substance?

Here are the top ten character traits of substance as I define it. You may have a different perspective. This is mine.

Top Ten Traits of a Woman of Substance

1. She is self-aware and knows her foundational values.

2. She sticks to her principles and never compromises on her integrity.

3. She is confident and believes in the unlimited potential of herself and her future.

4. She is diligent and knows progress lies in good solid habits and in taking action every day.

5. She is always learning, always questioning, whether she's nineteen or ninety-nine.

6. She is bold and assertive, and not afraid to do the right thing, even when others criticize or hate.

7. She is agile, does not sweat the small stuff, and knows failures are stepping-stones to success.

8. She is passionate about life and has a vision for the future that culminates in serving others as well as herself.

9. She takes care of her mental, physical, and emotional health, knowing without her health, nothing is possible.

10. She is compassionate and giving to others, and aspires to leave the world a better place than when she arrived on it.

"How does one become a butterfly? You have to want to learn to fly so much that you are willing to give up being a caterpillar."
Trina Paulus

YOUR DEFINITION OF SUCCESS

We each have our personal interpretation of what success means.

No definition is right or wrong. None of us have the same aspirations. How we think of progress can depend on our perceptions, experiences, and current circumstances.

While some of us may believe owning a multi-million-dollar waterfront mansion is the pinnacle of success, others may consider paying rent that month to be their greatest achievement. Some may fervently think Kim Kardashian espouses greatness while for others it's the late great Mother Teresa who does.

So, how do you define success?

Write your thoughts here. Keep these answers in the back of your mind as we go through this book.

I define success as:
1.
2.
3.
4.
5.

"None is more impoverished than the one who has no gratitude. Gratitude is a currency that we can mint for ourselves, and spend without fear of bankruptcy."
Fred De Witt Van Amburgh

BE GRATEFUL

Several years ago, I watched a foreign journalist interview a girl in a tattered blue dress, living in a refugee camp. His first question to her was, if she could have anything, *anything*, in the world, what would it be?

What was the little girl's response? "To stay alive."

Her answer broke my heart. I wish we didn't live in a world where the ambition of a young girl—or any child—is to survive. I wish we lived in a world where all children could aspire to be as happy and successful as you and I have the privilege of hoping and actually becoming.

The truth is nearly half of the world's population lives on less than $2.50 a day, and among them are one billion children.

Your prospects are dim if you're an illiterate woman scraping together a living in an Indian slum or if you're a young gay man living under a punitive regime in the Middle East. Life isn't easy even in first-world cities for those who live on the streets, fighting addiction and poverty.

In such challenging circumstances, it's difficult to think beyond the next day. Like the little girl in the refugee camp, there are many people on Earth whose sole goal is merely to live another day.

Knowing this, how can we not feel grateful? How can we not do everything in our power to make use of the good fortune we have?

You've been lucky to have had at least a primary education, most likely for free, that enables you to read this book. You have the means to buy a book and perhaps even an electronic device to read it on. You're fortunate to have the time to read rather than anxiously worry about how you'll feed your family tomorrow.

Your biggest conundrum right now might be to decide between finishing this book or digging into that leftover ice cream tub in the fridge and binge-watch another Netflix show. Yes, that's a tough decision. But a truly first world one. (Personally—and I'm biased—I'd leave the fridge and remote control alone and stick with this book for now.)

So, how many ways can we count how lucky we are?

Let's do that right now. That ice cream tub will still be there when you're done with this exercise. Promise.

I am grateful for:
1.
2.
3.
4.
5.

"Greatness is not measured by what a man or woman accomplishes, but by the opposition he or she has overcome to reach his goals."
Dorothy Height

TAKE OWNERSHIP

One of the biggest misconceptions we have about success is that it's a result of genetics, family name, physical ability, the size of our boobs or pecs, or some other quality external to our true self.

One of our biggest excuses is to blame someone else for our lack of progress and for where we're in life today.

How many people do you know attribute their failures to bad parents, a mean boss, disadvantaged backgrounds, an unfair society or even the government? How many people fail to live to their fullest capacity because they believe past circumstances have already decided their future?

As comforting as these sentiments may be (because it's always comforting to put the blame on someone else), these are defeatist, false beliefs.

The truth is far more empowering.

Our success is in our fully capable hands, regardless of where we came from or what experiences we've had.

No one has a crystal ball to predict the future, and I'd stay far away from anyone who says they can. (In fact, run away fast.) Even if predestination were to be true, we humans are intelligent and resourceful enough to overcome it and create our own desired future.

This is the most astounding characteristic of being born human. No other species has this amazing advantage.

You have a superpower and you may not have even known it.

MAKE LEMONADE

In my journeys across the world, I've met women and men who have survived situations most of us can't even fathom. Some have experienced horrific child abuse, brutal rapes, devastating illnesses, and even civil war. Yet, they persevered and rose above it all.

They grabbed on to life, took ownership of their attitude and made a conscious decision to move their lives forward, no matter what. They live meaningful and happy lives today because they never gave up on their convictions or hope for a brighter future.

They made sweet lemonade from the bitter fruits handed to them as arduous as that might have been. These courageous people are the true unsung heroes of our day.

In my travels, I've also met people who have had all the trappings of a good life including status, wealth, and privilege. They're the lucky ones, born to the right family in the right place.

Yet I've seen them squander their time. Everything they want is handed on a silver platter, so they have no inclination to reflect on their lives or the lives of others. I found them to be the most empty, apathetic, and the unhappiest people I've met.

The lesson I learned here is that despite our background or past, we have a choice.

We have a choice in how we see the world. We have a choice in what decisions we make in life. We have a choice in how we will move forward. All this is up to us.

MASTER THE POWER OF CHOICE

If you'd like to see real evidence of the power of choice, I'd suggest reading Dr. Viktor Frankl's *Man's Search for Meaning*.

This short but powerful story chronicles his time at a Second World War concentration camp. Amidst the horror, where he was violently robbed of all options available to a human being, he still believed he had a choice. And that was the choice of how he would respond to what was happening to him.

It was this book that woke me up from my own stupor and prompted me to stop stumbling aimlessly through life like a zombie and follow my passions.

If you have the fortune of living in a free and open society, you've got more freedoms than billions of other women and men around the world. You have more opportunities than ever before to design your future the way you see fit.

This doesn't mean it's going to be easy. You'll have to be brave. You'll have to exercise your willpower. You'll have to take action. And you'll have to work hard.

You may also have to make decisions that will make you unpopular. Yes, unpopular. Trying to win popularity contests is so high-school. We're adults now.

When you begin your heroine's journey, your peers, friends or family may discourage you, blame you, or even try to pull you down. They do this because your success will make them feel guilty for not taking action themselves.

All you can do is empathize, grow a thick skin and ignore the naysayers. Better yet, let them go. Get all negativity out of your life as soon as possible.

These decisions in life are yours to make, and yours alone.

It's your discretion to immerse yourself in toxic environments. Remember, it's your choice to never get off your couch. It's your preference to put unhealthy junk into your mouth—unless someone's force-feeding you with a gun to your head and in that case, you've got much bigger problems than this book can solve (I'd suggest dialing 9-1-1 fast).

In the same vein, it's in your total control to reach for healthier food options, to work out regularly, and to say a polite but firm "no" to anyone who treats you with disrespect.

Once you make a certain choice, knowing full well what you're doing (and our instincts are rarely wrong), you forfeit your right to blame. It makes little sense to complain as that's purely a waste of your precious energy. If you had wanted a different outcome, you needed to have made a different decision.

I know that sounds harsh, but no amount of excuses can help you escape the truth.

You may feel stuck right now in a bad situation, a crappy job or an unhappy relationship and see no way out. But what are your options?

You could waste your precious time blaming others for what they did or are doing to you. Or you could punish yourself for making mistakes in the past that got you to where you are today.

Blaming others only gives away your power back to them. Berating yourself saps your energy and stops you from getting ahead.

So, stop knocking on others. Learn from your mistakes. Be kind to yourself and keep your eyes focused on the road ahead. Make the right choices starting today.

"You'll never change your life until you change something you do daily. The secret of your success is found in your daily routine."
John C. Maxwell

A WAY OF LIFE

If you completed the first *Rebel Diva* workbook, *Your Rebel Dreams*, you'll have a life vision. If you then finished the second workbook in the series, *Your Rebel Plans*, you'll also have a plan to achieve that vision.

This means you know what treasures you seek in life and you have a roadmap to guide you toward your dreams. That's fantastic.

The final question is this: how can you design a fulfilling and healthy lifestyle that will get you to your vision faster?

For this, you must optimize your life and make it a healthy, harmonious and balanced one. Otherwise, you will find the journey a struggle. You may get distracted halfway through or even completely give up on your dreams.

As French novelist, Gustave Flaubert, said so beautifully, *"Be regular and orderly in your life, so that you may be violent and original in your work."*

When you create the right environment for yourself and adopt the right attitude and habits, your vision, however small or large, will invariably manifest itself. It has no choice but to come into being because you're doing everything to make it so.

Achieving your vision is not a short game. It's a way of living, thinking, and breathing. There's a philosophy to living a visionary life with no regrets.

So how can you create that way of life?

THE POWER OF HABITS

As mundane as it sounds, the road to your success lies in doing the little things right.

This means choosing healthy habits, cultivating them, and maintaining them every single day.

According to Brendon Burchard, a world-renowned author and high-performance coach, your vision and goals are like a car and your habits are its wheels. Without wheels—that is, your daily habits—your car won't roll. It can hardly move, if at all. In the same way, your habits play a powerful role in getting you rolling toward the future you wish to have.

Adopting a new habit means changing the way we do things. It means discipline. It means overcoming self-doubt and fear. It also means getting comfortable being uncomfortable, at least at the beginning.

I understand that none of these scenarios are attractive at first glance. Merely breathing the word *"habits"* makes most people scurry away like startled bunny rabbits. I know this because I was the biggest and scarediest rabbit of them all.

THE GREATEST PARADOX

There was a time in my life when I fell into a rut. I turned my mind off and stayed on the couch, eating potato chips and binge-watching yet another show (*Firefly*, anyone?) after spending a full day at a job I hated. The next morning, I hit the snooze button three times before stumbling out of bed, groaning and unhappy to start yet another meaningless day which I'd go through on autopilot.

It took a long time for me to realize that if I stayed on this path, a lifetime of opportunities would slip through my fingers. The ghosts of unachieved dreams would flit around my deathbed, mocking me. I'd wonder how I let my precious life steal away. The last breaths I'd take would be heavy with regret and tinged in disappointment.

What a way to die. I shudder with horror to even think of it. And this made me want to change and work toward my dreams.

One of the greatest paradoxes of life, though, is while everyone wants to realize their dreams, no one wants to do the very things that will get them off the couch and toward their vision. But it doesn't have to be this way.

BELIEVE IN YOURSELF

We can design a life that's fulfilling. One that brings us joy and makes our life vision come true.

Like everything else we tackled in the earlier workbooks, the impossible becomes possible when we break things down. Things get easier when we think of it as a game and track our progress from one level to the next.

But first, we must believe we can follow our vision. As Oprah has said many times, *"You don't become what you want, you become what you believe."* Belief in ourselves and our dreams is a primary step. The next is to take action.

WHAT'S NEXT

If you've gone through the first two books of the *Rebel Diva* series, you've come a long way to becoming a confident, cultivated woman who desires to make a positive difference in herself and those around her.

This third workbook will push you to the next stage of your growth adventure. In this book, we'll focus on building the right habits that will propel you toward your vision.

Your Rebel Life

"Our character is basically a composite of our habits. Because they are consistent, often unconscious patterns, they constantly, daily, express our character."
Stephen Covey

HABIT HACKS

There are no shortcuts to becoming successful.

I know what you're thinking. *Why the heck did I buy this book then?* I'm sorry I don't have an easy pill. No one does.

If anyone says they do, I'd walk away quickly. (Don't make eye contact or they'll hound you to part with your money so they can give you a jar of their snake oil wonder drug.)

One miracle, one tool or one solution—regardless of how sexy or awesome they may sound—won't create the life you desire. The magic to getting to your dreams lies in the everyday decisions you take, the daily choices you make. It's those little things, followed consistently in the long term, that will get you to a healthier, happier and successful you.

Do you know what happens to people who suddenly inherit large amounts of money or win the lottery? A majority lose their newfound wealth as swiftly as they gained it. What they were missing was a good understanding of their internal compass, a vision for their lives, and a set of good habits to guide their journey.

When we embrace the right habits, we create a supersonic highway to prosperity and happiness—one that's sustainable in the long run so we don't crash and burn.

But you don't need to overhaul your habits or your entire life overnight. That would exhaust you and, frankly, drive you nuts. You can start with one or two new habits, make incremental adjustments, and stay consistent every day. Little by little, you'll find your life improving and you'll see how you're getting closer to the treasures you seek.

Yes, it will take willpower and commitment (what doesn't? Other than eating ice cream from a tub.) But small changes are doable for anyone.

CHANGE IS EASIER THAN YOU THINK

Below are ten tips that will help you embrace new habits and keep them in the long-term.

Over the past few years, I applied these hacks in different intensities. They helped me transform from a bloated junk-food lover to a healthy vegan. They helped me create and manage a workout routine every morning. They also taught me how to get my work done every day though I no longer have a boss standing behind me with a disapproving frown on their face.

The changes I've adopted have made a world of difference in my health, weight, career, relationships, productivity, and outlook in life.

The techniques below are nothing more than ways to trick ourselves into doing things differently. They're so simple you'll wonder why I even mention them. It's because I want to show you that change is easier than you think.

So, let's begin.

1. FIND A TRIGGER

The fastest way to create a new habit is to identify a trigger that will remind you to take action naturally.

Let's take an easy example like flossing—recommended by dentists everywhere, but one few of us do. Come up with a trigger that will remind you to do this small act without trying too hard.

Think of flossing as simply the next step after dinner, or your next action after you read a story to your child at bedtime or any other activity that makes sense. Find the trigger action that will remind you of the upcoming habit action.

Then, write it on a post-it and stick it on your bathroom mirror. Tell your family about your new habit. Having this simple thought in the back of your mind will invariably push you into taking that next step as soon as the trigger is activated. If you do this enough times, you'll soon find that habit stick.

2. HOOK YOUR HABITS

If you already practice one habit, you can take it a step further by chaining a new habit to the existing one.

The reason most of us brush our teeth every evening is because we got this practice instilled in us in our young lives. We watched adults around us brush. Teachers may have talked about this basic hygiene practice or we may have been forbidden to go to bed before brushing. Either way, we created the habit and it stuck.

Now, if we can attach a new practice—flossing—to this current habit—brushing our teeth—we're giving ourselves a reminder that will create a chain of activity.

Hooking is like creating a trigger, except it's a forward trigger. As we put our toothbrush away, we can tell ourselves, "After I brush my teeth, I'll floss," or something to that effect. If we do this enough times, this second habit—flossing—will become ingrained. And we've created a new habit.

3. SET UP FOR SUCCESS

Another way to start a new habit is to set your environment up for success from the beginning.

For the flossing example, you can put your floss packet right next to your toothbrush. This way, you can't help but notice the floss and pick it up (and feel guilty if you don't).

If you're trying to convince yourself to go for an early morning run, put your running shoes and gear out the night before, so they're the first things you see when you get up. If you want to eat more fruit, as I do, leave a tangerine or apple on your desk every morning. If you want to drink more water, fill up your favorite mug or bottle and put it where you won't miss it.

Having all the necessary items in your line of vision at the right time and in the right place will remind you of your routine and make it easy to start.

This practice may seem awkward at first, but after a few weeks, you'll feel something is missing if you forget to leave your running shoes and gear (or your floss) out.

4. START SMALL

I started my morning exercises with five minutes of yoga. I took eight months to ramp it up to fifteen minutes, then another six months to add a ten-minute core exercise routine. Over several months, this turned into a daily thirty minutes of solid physical activity. After four years, I now have a full hour of yoga and physical exercise which primes me for the day, every single day.

All this from starting with five measly minutes.

How can anyone say no to just five? You can't make excuses and it seems silly not to carry through.

So start small. Begin with a few minutes of whatever you're trying to do. Increase it by five minutes the next month, then five more the following month, and so on. If you do this regularly, you'll achieve magic in no time.

5. MEASURE IT

Did you know that tracking a behavior is one of the best ways to solidify it? Once you keep track of your habits, it becomes difficult to slack.

Measure your progress and write it in a daily journal and the habit will get ingrained quickly. As a bonus, your motivation will also grow. Even if you're not naturally a competitive person, you'll try to beat or at least retain yesterday's numbers.

I found this to be the most effective hack by far to ingrain a new habit. I've used this to transform my sleeping, eating and workout practices, all areas I didn't think I could change.

6. STICK TO THIRTY DAYS

Studies have shown that you need to carry out an activity consistently for twenty to thirty days to make it a habit.

This depends on the activity and our own mindset, but thirty days is a reasonable amount of time to strive toward. So try one activity for a full month, without fail. If you feel like quitting, tell yourself, "It's just till the end of this month. That's not too long. I can do that."

Increase your odds further by thinking about the activity consciously, writing it down, scheduling it, setting alarms, or getting an accountability partner—whatever works for you.

Do one thing for thirty days and that will increase the chances you'll stick to the habit in the long-term.

7. FORGIVE YOURSELF

We're only human. We'll have days when we forget to carry through with a habit. We'll get sick or get thrown off by an emergency. That's normal.

The worst response we can give when this happens is to blame ourselves. Never beat yourself up because you missed or forgot a day or two. Instead, acknowledge the slip and tell yourself you'll do it the next day. Then move on.

Treat yourself gently, and remember, it's what you do the majority of the time that matters.

8. FOCUS ON TODAY

The most profound yet simple lesson I've learned to date is the power of now.

We can't do anything about what happened yesterday because that time has passed. Neither can we do anything about tomorrow because it hasn't happened yet. (If you don't believe me, try it and you'll see.) All we have is right now.

It's in this exact moment we can do something, *anything*. So let's stop wasting time, energy, and emotions on things we can't affect, and instead pay attention to what we can accomplish right now.

Pay attention to what you can do now. And focus wholly on that.

9. CELEBRATE SUCCESSES

Remember to celebrate each of your wins, no matter how big or small. In fact, think of how you'll celebrate before you even start a new habit. This way, you'll have an incentive to look forward to.

Use rewards as positive reinforcement. They'll boost your morale and motivate you to extend the habit or even take on another good habit. Then another and another. Before you know it, you'll have created a shiny new you.

See? This is exactly why you needed to save that tub of ice cream in the fridge.

10. DO IT FOR OTHERS

A recent study done on marathon runners revealed an interesting fact about why we do what we do. They found a fundamental distinction between those who ran for a cause greater than themselves and those who ran solely for themselves.

Many runners who signed up because they wanted the medal, the status, the weight loss from training, or to have something to brag about at the water cooler the next morning didn't show up or pulled out before the race even began. Those who were running to raise funds for a nonprofit they cared about, or because they made a promise to a loved one who was sick, all showed up and finished the race.

The lesson here is you're more likely to stick to an activity when you're doing it for others. You don't want to let them down, so the incentive to persevere is stronger.

As you look at the habits listed in the upcoming chapters, ask yourself why this life habit is important to you. Then ask yourself who you'd like to inspire or motivate through your actions. That will be a powerful motivator for you.

"To live is the rarest thing in the world. Most people exist, that is all."
Oscar Wilde

THE TEN PILLARS OF OUR LIVES

There are many ways to slice and dice our modern lives. This workbook breaks down the most important facets of life using what we, in a normal course of the day, think about, talk about, and engage in.

The ten pillars listed here should capture the main facets of your life. But if you find some pieces are missing given your particular lifestyle, apply the concepts here to build up those areas.

The ten life pillars are:

> 1. Feeling Well - Our Environment Health: The surrounding environment, the people we spend time with, and the information we immerse ourselves in.
>
> 2. Sleeping Well - Our Rejuvenation Health: How much rest we give our brains and bodies to recharge every day.
>
> 3. Moving Well - Our Physical Health: Our physical state, and how healthy and fit our bodies are.
>
> 4. Eating Well - Our Nutrition Health: The nutrition we put into our bodies and its effect on us.
>
> 5. Learning Well - Our Knowledge Health: How we learn and retain new skills and knowledge, despite our age.
>
> 6. Working Well - Our Career Health: The work we do every day and how it feeds our souls as much as our wallets.

7. Investing Well - Our Wealth Health: Our relationship with money and how we manage our finances.

8. Thinking Well - Our Mental Health: The state of our minds and our mental well-being.

9. Loving Well - Our Relationship Health: The strength of our relationships with ourselves as well as others.

10. Playing Well - Our Spirit Health: How we see life and whether we can perceive it as a journey of exploration and unlimited potential.

A HOLISTIC VIEW

Once you go through all the sections in this workbook, you'll have a framework to design a holistic life. This will be the foundation for your success. But it's important to remember that these pillars don't exist in a vacuum. You need all of them working together to hold you up high.

If your career's flying high but your relationships are suffering, that will eventually compromise your work and jeopardize your future. If you've got all the main areas of your life figured out but your work environment is toxic, you'll be susceptible to illnesses or even burnout.

So, eating jalapeno potato chips, chocolate chip cookies, and salted pickles at every meal while you manage a daily workout regimen won't cut it. Aside from being a terrible combination of tastes (unless you have pregnancy cravings, which is a completely different affair altogether), this food won't create a healthy body, however hard you exercise.

Conversely, when you eat right, get a good night's rest, work out regularly, surround yourself with encouraging people in a positive environment, and look at life as an amazing adventure, you'll boost the health of all other areas.

But you can't make wholesale change at once. That could overwhelm you and even discourage you from taking action. Work brick by brick—building one small habit every month. As they say, Rome wasn't built in a day. This is your *life* we're talking about.

You're creating a life of health and happiness so you can get to your dreams. Take your time. Enjoy the journey. Know you're doing the right thing.

HOW TO USE THIS BOOK

You probably already figured out that this book is not meant to be read like a normal book.

Each section, except for this introduction, stands alone in its own right. You won't miss anything by picking the parts that call out to you the most.

Schedule an hour per section to read through the main tips and give yourself time to do the exercises and synthesize the lessons. Allow yourself at least a week in between each section to practice what you learned.

Whatever you do, don't read this book in one sitting. Choose the life pillars that are most important to you and read those sections first. Focus on one section per week, not more.

Think of the time you dedicate to each section as your *me-time* and set aside that time to show some good care for yourself.

Good luck!

CAUTION

This is a layperson's guide to optimizing the most important areas of your life. This should not be construed as professional advice, or medical, psychological, legal, financial, nutritional, or other such counsel.

Each of the life pillars explained here deserves its own book, or several, to do it justice.

To keep this workbook to a manageable reading size, the techniques shared here are the highlights of each topic. The aim is to give you practical and simplified tips you can apply quickly. A list of extra resources, books, videos, and thought-leaders is provided at the back of this book if you'd like to delve deeper into any of these life facets.

"Buckle up, and know that it's going to be a tremendous amount of work, but embrace it."
Tory Burch

PRIORITIZE YOUR LIFE PILLARS

Each section in this book will require sixty minutes of quiet time to read, digest, and answer the questions.

Look at the areas of your life you find most challenging right now. Prioritize these and go to these sections first.

If all you do is tackle these areas, that's a great start. You can always come back to the remaining sections later on to check how you can enhance those areas further.

When you get to the exercises in each section, set an annual goal for that area. Come up with at least one activity you'll try out that month.

Then, come back to this book at the end of the month to see how well you did and set another activity for the following month.

If you can stick to this process consistently every month, you'll see enormous progress in your life.

Prioritize your sections here. Check the sections you want to start with.

MY ENVIRONMENT	
Section 1 Feel Well: My Environmental Health	Date:

MY HEALTH	
Section 2 Sleep Well: My Rejuvenation Health	Date:
Section 3 Move Well: My Physical Health	Date:
Section 4 Eat Well: My Nutrition Health	Date:

MY VOCATION	
Section 5 Learn Well: My Knowledge Health	Date:
Section 6 Work Well: My Career Health	Date:
Section 7 Invest Well: My Wealth Health	Date:

MY SPIRIT	
Section 8 Think Well: My Mental Health	Date:
Section 9 Love Well: My Relationship Health	Date:
Section 10 Play Well: My Spirit Health	Date:

LET'S BEGIN

Have you got an hour scheduled in? Have you told everyone this is your *me-time*?

Wonderful.

Now, find a cozy spot to curl up in with this book, your favorite cup of tea, coffee, or beverage of choice, and a purple pen (I love purple but you may prefer another color!).

And that's all you need. Plus an open mind.

The journey to achieving your dream life is much easier than you think.

A SHORT MEDITATION

So, are you now in your favorite spot with a hot cup of tea, coffee, or maybe an ice tea?

Get comfy. Set your book down, and put aside the cup and pen for a moment. Sit still with both feet on the ground, back straight but soft, arms to your sides, and your body relaxed but alert.

Close your eyes.

Now, take five deep and slow breaths. Breathe in through your nose and out through your mouth. Feel your diaphragm expand and contract as you breathe deeply. Concentrate on your breath and feel it coming in and going out.

Make your breaths long and slow. Breathe in. And breathe out. Feel the air come in through your nostrils and fill your insides. Then feel the whoosh of your breath as it leaves you. Keep breathing slowly, gently, mindfully.

Take your time and take as many deep breaths as you need to settle yourself. This will help you relax and clear your mind of any mental debris that could cloud your thinking. When you're done with the meditation, sit back and turn the page.

Read the tips and answer the questions that show up, one by one. Be honest with yourself. Indulge in yourself. Put down responses that make you smile. You don't have to fill in all the blanks, only what you want.

You can start each section of this book with this short meditation to get you in the zone. And remember you should celebrate every time you finish a section!

PRINT EXERCISES IN BOOK

Download the PDF worksheet booklet for *Your Rebel Life*.

This booklet includes worksheets for all the exercises in this book. You can print them, write your answers directly on them, pin them up if you'd like and refer to them every day.

Tap on the link below to download your free private copy.

Your Rebel Life Worksheet Booklet

https://www.rebeldivas.com/rebel-life-page/

SECTION ONE

FEEL WELL

Environment Health

"Never underestimate the power of dreams and the influence of the human spirit. We are all the same in this notion: The potential for greatness lives within each of us."

Wilma Rudolph

"It takes a great deal of courage to stand up to your enemies, but even more to stand up to your friends."
J.K. Rowling

FEEL WELL

Our Environment Health

WHAT I'VE LEARNED ABOUT FEELING WELL

Jim Rohn, legendary motivational speaker and author, said, "You're the average of the five people you surround yourself with."

At more than one point in my life, I've looked around and shuddered at the thought of becoming the average of those I was with. As a child growing up in a toxic environment, I had no way to change this unless I ran away from home. I seriously contemplated it more than once, but frequent international moves made this a difficult and a dangerous thing to do.

AN EXAMPLE

Later on, as an adult, I got mired in a similar situation, surrounded by colleagues and friends with whom I had little in common. It wasn't as bad as my childhood, but it held me back and made me miserable.

Half of my coworkers hated Monday mornings, kept their heads down, did what they could, and relished counting their days till retirement. Their speech and body language silently said, "I'm just another cog in the wheel."

At the end of one dull meeting, one of them turned to me at the back of a gray boardroom and whispered, "Only thing that's keeping me going is I'm one year closer to being free." So I asked her how many more years she had till she could retire. Her answer—said with head bowed, the lines on her face deepening—was "twenty-six."

I was flabbergasted. She had relegated a quarter of a century to tolerating a dismal existence. I didn't say anything, but that was the most depressing conversation I've had in my working life.

The other half of my colleagues seemed to enjoy steamrolling over others. I saw them squeeze the sweat and tears from their teams and leave dead bodies littered in their wake. I saw them fawn over senior managers, flattering them to get the next promotion. I regularly saw decisions made based on personal and organizational politics. In these workplaces, no one took responsibility for mistakes. How many of you know what I'm talking about?

This culture is not at all uncommon in large, entrenched bureaucracies. I worked in this climate across several organizations for many years, seeing little integrity or leadership. I was so disheartened that whenever a senior manager spoke with passion and authenticity, I went home feeling elated. But this happened rarely, and those feelings didn't last.

It took me years to figure out what this environment was doing to me.

I was slowly absorbing the qualities I saw. I too began to detest Mondays and take on a dull look on my face. I became hard-nosed about getting projects done to get recognized by senior management, to the point I stepped on the toes of my teammates. Sometimes I stomped on entire feet without realizing or even apologizing (if any of you are reading this, I'm truly sorry).

MAKING CHANGE

It was a series of life-changing events on the personal front that shocked me awake to the poison I was drinking. So, before I transformed further into something I didn't want to be, I quit. And that was the best decision I made in a decade and a half.

Why is it so challenging to make these transformations? Why is it so difficult to change our environments? No one had chained me to my job, but I stayed on for years feeling as miserable as a wet puppy tied to a short leash.

We, as humans, are highly susceptible to what and who surrounds us and are always tuned into our environments. This subconscious trait comes from our tribal ancestors who roamed the savannah lands, always on the lookout for a prehistoric hyena or tiger lurking in the shadows behind a bush. They had to generalize complicated images, be prepared for worst-case scenarios, and not put their necks out.

While we no longer encounter primordial carnivores in our neighborhoods or workplaces (some of you may disagree, but stay with me here), we still worry about danger. Our brains have such a strong negativity bias it's difficult to rise above our circumstances and push ourselves forward.

But we can do this.

We don't have to exist in a frightened and constantly ready-to-flee state. We're more than capable of changing our environment or creating new ones to alter the trajectory of our future. This is in our hands.

CREATING OUR ZONE

Our personal environments are similar to the zones a city might establish for different neighborhoods.

Municipalities are zoned for commercial use, residences, schooling, and parking with strict bylaws that enforce these boundaries. Similar to cities which create zones to encourage growth and enhance the well-being of their citizens, we too can create personal zones around us that foster what we want—good health, harmony, and happiness—while keeping out negativity, hostility, and unacceptable behavior with the same rigor as a city's bylaws.

The resigned despair on my colleague's face, the one who had twenty-six years to go before retiring, was heartbreaking. She was immersed in an environment whose values were diametrically opposed to what she held in her heart. I was in the same boat and the day I broke free, I felt intoxicatingly happy.

We all desire joy in life. We all want to laugh, love, learn, flourish, and get acknowledged for who we are and what we do. Above all, we want to live true to ourselves.

The good news is we can find and create positive spaces that align with our principles. These are places that make us feel thrilled to be alive and make us show up every day as the best version of ourselves.

So, how do we do that?

After four stock-taking questions on the next page, we'll move straight to a practical exercise that will help you create the environment you desire.

THE STATE OF MY ENVIRONMENT HEALTH TODAY

First, four key stock-taking questions.

1. How are you doing in this pillar of your life right now?

- ○ Great! I'm Super Woman at this.
- ○ Okay. I know things can be better but it's not too bad.
- ○ Not too well. I wish things were different.
- ○ Meh. I'm not at all interested in this area.

2. Why is this area of your life important to you right now?

3. Who around you will get inspired when you start taking care of this part of your life?

4. What is your one main goal for enhancing your environment health this year?

We'll talk about specific tips and actions you can take on the next page, but for now, set an overarching goal for this area of your life for this year.

"The first step toward success is taken when you refuse to be a captive of the environment in which you first find yourself."
Mark Caine

MY ENVIRONMENT HEALTH

TEN TIPS

1. UPGRADE YOUR SPACE

Let's begin with an easy question. What does your space look like at work?

Is your environment organized and clean, or is it in total disarray? What about the smells, the sounds, and the colors in your surrounding area? Do they give you headaches, or do they bring a sense of serenity? Does your space make you feel depressed and gloomy, or does it inspire and motivate you?

Some folks can work miracles amid chaos, but most of us need a clear physical space to feel calm and become productive. If you can't work in a mess, remove the things that bring out any negative emotions in you.

Throw away magazines or papers you will never read. Give away anything that's been collecting dust, like that pile of cheap conference promo giveaways. Do you really need another lanyard, logo button, or plastic cup? That's clutter you don't want around you.

A clean space will have fewer distractions to pull you away from your work and fewer messes to stumble over. It will help you focus on what's most important and get more done.

To boost your mood and stimulate your creativity, bring in a plant to your office. Or get a motivational poster, add a cushion for your chair or place a pretty rug under your desk. Put on your favorite music and wear headphones if you're in an open area. If you're lucky to work at home, burn incense or light a candle to allow good energy to flow around you. None of this will cost you much.

Speaking of home, clean up your bedroom, kitchen counters, and cupboards. Yes, even your cupboards. This may be challenging if you've got toddlers in your household. But do the best you can to create a peaceful, positive and productive environment that stimulates and uplifts you, not distracts you.

These little things matter.

2. ELIMINATE STRESSORS

If listening or reading to the nightly news distresses you, turn it off. Stop reading magazines or articles that raise your blood pressure. There's a fine line between staying informed and wallowing in the negativity the media feeds to us every day. Find that line and don't cross it for your own sanity.

If you get distracted by all the pings and rings from your electronic devices, turn off all notifications or the Internet altogether until you're finished with the task at hand. I've permanently turned off all notifications on my phone, other than calls from certain key numbers. At the end of the day, I check all my important inboxes to catch up and reply as needed.

Prioritize your time, or your life will be overtaken by mindless and mostly useless matters disguised as urgent calls to actions.

If commuting is a necessary evil, ask yourself how you can turn it around and make it into an activity you look forward to. Bring along your favorite music playlist, a podcast from a course or program you don't have time to listen to. Ask a good friend to carpool with you so you'll have company. Your commute might even transform into a pleasant and productive part of your day.

If you find it aggravating to work in loud and busy places, find a quiet boardroom, or go to the library and avoid busy coffee shops. If you're always getting interrupted and can't finish your work, put up a do-not-disturb sign for a specific period to let everyone know this is your thinking/ planning/

reading/ writing/ researching quiet time. Add a smiley face to make it friendly. :)

If you explain your needs to your colleagues and family politely, most people will understand and respect you. They may even copy your idea.

As a former manager, I've been open to colleagues working from home, especially when the work requires intense concentration. I've accommodated busy moms and dads working from home during school holidays or when their kids were sick. Most leaders I know are reasonable and open-minded as long as no one abuses this courtesy. A friendly chat with the boss is all that's needed most times.

If your work environment, bosses, or colleagues bring out anxiety in you on a regular basis, perhaps it's time to rethink how you spend most of your days. Find work that brings more joy and meaning to your life. This is easier said than done, but ask yourself if you want to live your entire life fighting off negativity.

On the home front, if certain family members or neighbors bother you, keep your distance. There's no need to meet with them every time they ask. Minimize your interactions and remain friendly. Remember, if they give you a guilt trip for not hanging out with them, that's one more reason to stay away. Far away.

Take all these stressors into account when you look for your next home, neighborhood, job or contract. It's not easy or cheap to make wholesale changes, so whenever you're in that position, take advantage of it. Minimize stressful triggers from the start.

3. FIND YOUR IDEAL ENVIRONMENT

We spend a majority of our hours at work. That environment can have a significant impact on our physical and mental health in the long run. If you'll be seeking employment soon or are on the verge of changing jobs, this is a good time to ask yourself what type of workspace suits you best.

Why not make a list of what you're looking for and ferret those places out? Consider your ideal location, work hours, physical space, lighting, noise levels, size and type of teams, core management values, office traditions and culture, availability of child care, and even the possibility of bringing your puppy to work (if that's a need).

Create a picture of your dream workplace. Look around to find which companies already embody these features. Narrow them down to create a short list. Then see if you can speak with people who work in these places to learn more about their environments.

Never be afraid to ask questions in an interview about organization culture. If your potential employers hem and haw or dodge your questions, you'll know they don't want to divulge something or didn't give it much thought—two red flags that will tell you this may not be the ideal place for you.

Does this seem like a lot of effort? If it does, think about how much time you'll be dedicating to go to this workplace every single day. This proactive research is well worth it.

If you can't find your ideal work environment, perhaps that's a signal for you to create it. Yes, build it yourself!

Entrepreneurship is not for everyone, but there are many options to explore these days, from part-time work to remote working to job sharing to freelancing and more. Don't restrict yourself to the traditional definitions of employment.

The world is changing and technology is our friend. Use this in your favor.

4. TRUST YOUR GUT

Always, always, always trust your instincts.

Your body will send you warning signals well before your brain has the time to analyze the situation, gather the information, and make a conscious decision.

Have you ever gone on a date and throughout dinner felt uncomfortable even though the guy or girl sitting across from you seemed perfectly normal and even a great catch? Something in you knows you'll regret it if you agree to another date. Yet, how many of us say yes to be nice or because we fervently wish it would turn out okay, although our gut says otherwise?

Most times, we won't see any logical reason to feel uneasy, but every time I've ignored those feelings, I've regretted it. Massively.

Several years ago I was scheduled to meet a high-profile manager in an organization I badly wanted to work for. It was a job that would catapult my career and I was over the moon about being called for the interview. But as soon as I walked into that manager's office, a sense of dread washed over me.

I kept my composure and gave her my most professional smile, but the feeling got stronger when I reached out to shake her hand. Something about her demeanor, posture, and tone was telling me something I needed to know.

A few days later, I learned how badly she mistreated her employees. Many had resigned, taken early retirement, or gone on sick leave. HR was dealing with a litany of legal grievances, and many called it a hellish place to work in. I'm glad I figured this out before I decided to join the team.

If certain people leave you feeling uncomfortable, take note of what your body's telling you. If you get bad vibes every time you see them, there's truth hidden in those feelings which you need to investigate further.

This doesn't mean becoming paranoid. It means keeping your eyes open and being aware of your feelings as well as your surroundings.

Listen to your instincts. They're wiser than you think.

5. HAVE STANDARDS

One of my favorite quotes from Oprah is, "You can either tolerate low standards for yourself and those around you, or you can up your standards and up your life, up your lifestyle and up your happiness."

Tony Robbins agrees. He says: "Your life is a reflection of your standards, and what you're willing to tolerate."

These are powerful statements because they mean we can design the life we desire. Our future is in our hands. Our happiness depends on the standards we uphold. How empowering is that?

But most of us, sadly, don't recognize this power within us.

Don't we all have that lovely high-school girlfriend who was so concerned about being lonely she connected with any man who came her way? But all she did was invite unnecessary complications into her life. What if, instead, she sought out partners who were caring, respectful, intelligent, and have high standards themselves? Wouldn't that have led to a happier and more peaceful future for her, even though it may have taken time to find the right person?

So, what standards do you live by?

If you have a habit of saying to yourself or to others, "I'm lazy and I'm always procrastinating," you'll continue on that route. You've confirmed to yourself that you accept little from yourself. So, you may not get much done and to top it off, you'll feel bad about yourself.

You could turn this around by saying, "I believe in myself and I will finish what I started." This will manifest in a very different future, one where you'll accomplish your goals and feel good about yourself.

As Henry Ford was known to say, "Whether you think you can, or you think you can't, you're right." He was right.

So, why not go for the gold? Look at all the areas of your life, from your health to your career, finances, and relationships, and up your standards today.

Remember, nothing happens from wishing or hoping. Once you identify a set of higher standards for yourself, you must act. You'll soon attract more people, events, and situations that meet those elevated standards.

Plus, there's a nice side effect to this.

When you show the world who you are and what you're not willing to tolerate, you'll find others will respect you more. Your credibility will get a boost, and your ability to persuade others will expand. This is a great place to be.

6. BE CAREFUL WHO GETS CLOSE TO YOU

Whenever we get close to people with little self-discipline or emotional control, or those who are self-absorbed and play mind games, we invite all that drama into our own lives.

Other people's unhealthy physical and mental habits will impact us directly or indirectly if we let them.

Be especially wary of people who call themselves your friends but who always leave a slightly bad taste in your mouth. Maybe it's their backhanded compliments, put-downs, side jabs or advice that's supposed to be "for your own good."

Unsolicited advice rarely comes from a place of good intentions, especially when the person speaking doesn't know your full story or hasn't had similar experiences to you. Such folks give advice to make themselves feel better. Their words are only a reflection of their own insecurities. You can nod and smile, but let them go as quickly as you can.

This is not a call to judge others indiscriminately, but to be aware of how another person's personality, thinking, and actions can impact your peace of mind.

Think about the kind of people, based on character and personality, you'll allow into your inner circle. Make sure the boundaries are clear.

Most times, when we ignore another person's bad behavior, we give them permission to continue hurting themselves and us. But letting go can be difficult if they're close family members. At least, distance yourself to protect your own mental sanity and good health.

Motivational speaker Les Brown likes to say improving yourself is a full-time job. If you feel bad about letting people go or believe you can change them for the better, remember you're already busy working on yourself. You can't fix another adult human being. Neither is it your task to do so.

As much as we like to think we can change those around us, it's a futile and frustrating exercise that will pull us into a foxhole we'll have a hard time extricating ourselves from.

Let others go on their journey of self-discovery on their own time. Giving them the space to do so will be the most empathetic thing you can do.

Seek friends who think positively and who're cultivating healthy habits in their minds, bodies, and spirits. Look for people who show integrity and honesty in their words and in their behavior. Scout out those people who do work you admire. Find new friends who have your best interests at heart and who will cheer you on without envying you or losing confidence themselves.

Who we surround ourselves with matters more than we think. Valuable friends aren't easy to find, but they're well worth the search. You will first need to make space for them by letting go of those who no longer belong in your life. Then be patient. They will come.

7. MAKE TIME FOR GOOD PEOPLE

Once we find the right friends, we must nurture those relationships and let them know we appreciate having them in our lives.

Just as I'm quick to walk away from negative environments, I'm as fast to affirm a good friendship by sending thank-you notes or flowers, giving compliments and lifting their moods, inviting them for tea and supper, and supporting them and cheering for them whenever they're in need.

We get sucked into the busyness of life and forget to spend time with the good people around us. How many colleagues do you know who get so caught up at work they miss their daughter's football game or their son's recital? We take the closest people around us for granted and only miss them when they're gone.

So, make a conscious decision to hang out with your loved ones and good friends on a regular basis and schedule it in so you don't forget and lose touch.

Studies have shown that a supportive and loving community, whether it's family or friendships, is a hallmark for health and longevity. Good friends are good medicine. Treat them like gold.

8. SEEK HAPPY PLACES

Akin to finding the right friends, we also need to seek places that bring us joy.

Make a list of the venues you like to visit and go there often. Maybe it's a library or a Latin dance club. You may enjoy being at the gym, the local swimming pool or on a bicycle track. Or perhaps it's a classroom or the local animal shelter.

Find your happy places and look for them in your neighborhood. These are also where the good people you seek hang out.

If you're fortunate to live near nature, visit it often. Studies have shown that immersing yourself in natural habitats boosts happiness and significantly reduces your levels of stress hormones.

Visit a flower garden, a vineyard, a beach, a forest or if you're very lucky, the foot of a majestic snowcapped mountain. If you live in the middle of a large urban area, seek out city parks or local aquariums to get back in touch with nature. Even a few minutes staring at fish swimming in a tank can do wonders for your mood and stress.

Beautiful places are all around us. There was a time in my childhood where all I had was a single tree in a bare yard that backed onto a nuclear power plant somewhere in sub-Saharan Africa. Though it was a dismal place, that lovely little tree under which I sat to do my homework every day was my paradise. Even in that desolate neighborhood, I found my happy place.

Open your eyes and spot the wonderful places around you.

9. CONSIDER WHERE YOU LIVE

Don't limit yourself to your immediate surroundings.

Think about the part of town you're in. What's your neighborhood like? Is it a noisy, harried place? Is it prone to crime and violence? Who are your neighbors? How do they treat each other?

These are important questions to ask if you're serious about creating a good life for yourself and your loved ones.

You can change your home, albeit at a much greater cost and time commitment than bringing a plant to your office. You'll need to plan for it. It may be one of the most difficult decisions you make in your lifetime, but people have made wholesale moves since the beginning of time. It's the main reason millions emigrate every year—to find a better environment for their families and their future.

As an immigrant myself, I know that living in the country I'm in now gives me more economic advantages and personal success than I could have ever imagined as a child. I started my twenties with zero connections and cash. Given that, I'd never have reached the standard of living I enjoy today if I lived in places where conflict, corruption, and misogyny are rampant.

Some of the most successful self-made millionaires grew up in challenging and even dangerous and violent neighborhoods. They upgraded their lives only after they propelled themselves out of these environments.

Don't accept your current environment, city or even country as the only place to live. You have options. It's up to you to take advantage of them if you want to change your life for the better.

10. STAY MINDFUL

I can already hear you ask, *Okay, but what in the heck can I do if I'm stuck in a bad environment and can't get out?*

Being mindful is probably one of the most effective ways to control your emotions when you're immersed in a painful place. I know that's not what you wanted to hear, but stay with me.

Our brains are buzzing at a rate of 70,000 thoughts per day. Given our negativity bias, you can bet your bottom dollar most of these thoughts aren't expansive, positive, or uplifting.

You may be anxious about a difficult conversation you had earlier, worried about an upcoming meeting with your boss, or tearing your hair out at a life dilemma you're facing. What if you could reduce your head chatter and take a few seconds to concentrate on the smallest thing you're doing right now?

If you're making a cup of tea, really listen to the sound of the water boiling. Notice the color of the tea in your cup. If you're writing a report, really get into the premise and do the best job you can on it. If you're talking to someone, show them you're listening, ask them questions, and give attention to their body language and their words.

If you can live in the moment, it will be like a short meditation that will soothe your mind, regardless of what's going on around you.

When you get into this quiet zone every once in a while, it can do wonders to bring calm and peace even if things are a little crazy around you.

Then, with that clearer mind, you can figure out how to remove yourself from the bad situation altogether.

It will take time. Be patient with yourself.

THE HABIT MAKER

Let's Make These Stick

Pick one idea from the tips list and try it out for one month. Do this for thirty days and see how you do. Then, if you can, try a new one next month.

So, what is *one* action you'll take to incorporate environmental fitness into your life this month?

Go back to the annual goal you set at the start of this section and make sure the activity you choose links to your goals.

Set January Activity:
Track the Activity: Check back at the end of the month to see how well you did
○ Great! I was Super Woman at this.   ○ Good. I managed this most of the time.   ○ Okay, I guess. I know I can get better.   ○ Not so well. So, maybe I need to try this again. Who said you have to get it right the first time.
How can I improve next month?

Set February Activity:

Track the Activity: Check back at the end of the month to see how well you did

- ○ Great! I was Super Woman at this.
- ○ Good. I managed this most of the time.
- ○ Okay, I guess. I know I can get better.
- ○ Not so well. So, maybe I need to try this again. Who said you have to get it right the first time.

How can I improve next month?

Set March Activity:

Track the Activity: Check back at the end of the month to see how well you did

- ○ Great! I was Super Woman at this.
- ○ Good. I managed this most of the time.
- ○ Okay, I guess. I know I can get better.
- ○ Not so well. So, maybe I need to try this again. Who said you have to get it right the first time.

How can I improve next month?

Set April Activity:
Track the Activity: Check back at the end of the month to see how well you did
○ Great! I was Super Woman at this. ○ Good. I managed this most of the time. ○ Okay, I guess. I know I can get better. ○ Not so well. So, maybe I need to try this again. Who said you have to get it right the first time.
How can I improve next month?

Set May Activity:
Track the Activity: Check back at the end of the month to see how well you did
○ Great! I was Super Woman at this. ○ Good. I managed this most of the time. ○ Okay, I guess. I know I can get better. ○ Not so well. So, maybe I need to try this again. Who said you have to get it right the first time.
How can I improve next month?

Set June Activity:

Track the Activity: Check back at the end of the month to see how well you did

- ○ Great! I was Super Woman at this.
- ○ Good. I managed this most of the time.
- ○ Okay, I guess. I know I can get better.
- ○ Not so well. So, maybe I need to try this again. Who said you have to get it right the first time.

How can I improve next month?

Set July Activity:

Track the Activity: Check back at the end of the month to see how well you did

- ○ Great! I was Super Woman at this.
- ○ Good. I managed this most of the time.
- ○ Okay, I guess. I know I can get better.
- ○ Not so well. So, maybe I need to try this again. Who said you have to get it right the first time.

How can I improve next month?

Set August Activity:

Track the Activity: Check back at the end of the month to see how well you did

- ○ Great! I was Super Woman at this.
- ○ Good. I managed this most of the time.
- ○ Okay, I guess. I know I can get better.
- ○ Not so well. So, maybe I need to try this again. Who said you have to get it right the first time.

How can I improve next month?

Set September Activity:

Track the Activity: Check back at the end of the month to see how well you did

- ○ Great! I was Super Woman at this.
- ○ Good. I managed this most of the time.
- ○ Okay, I guess. I know I can get better.
- ○ Not so well. So, maybe I need to try this again. Who said you have to get it right the first time.

How can I improve next month?

Set October Activity:

Track the Activity: Check back at the end of the month to see how well you did

- ○ Great! I was Super Woman at this.
- ○ Good. I managed this most of the time.
- ○ Okay, I guess. I know I can get better.
- ○ Not so well. So, maybe I need to try this again. Who said you have to get it right the first time.

How can I improve next month?

Set November Activity:

Track the Activity: Check back at the end of the month to see how well you did

- ○ Great! I was Super Woman at this.
- ○ Good. I managed this most of the time.
- ○ Okay, I guess. I know I can get better.
- ○ Not so well. So, maybe I need to try this again. Who said you have to get it right the first time.

How can I improve next month?

Set December Activity:
Track the Activity: Check back at the end of the month to see how well you did
○ Great! I was Super Woman at this. ○ Good. I managed this most of the time. ○ Okay, I guess. I know I can get better. ○ Not so well. So, maybe I need to try this again. Who said you have to get it right the first time.
How can I improve next month?

SO, HOW DO YOU FEEL?

That's the end of this section. What do you think of the answers you gave here? If something wasn't captured in this section but you want to get it out of your system, this is the place to do so.

_____

_____

_____

_____

_____

_____

_____

_____

_____

_____

BREAK

Fantastic work!

You want to learn these concepts for the long-term, so there's no use cramming and going through this book all at once. If you read a chapter, do the exercises and take a break, you'll absorb the ideas and come up with even better solutions.

This is a good time to take a break and let all this percolate in your brain while you do other things. Come back in a week to move on to the next habit.

Do this every time you see this break page.

SECTION TWO
SLEEP WELL

Rejuvenation Health

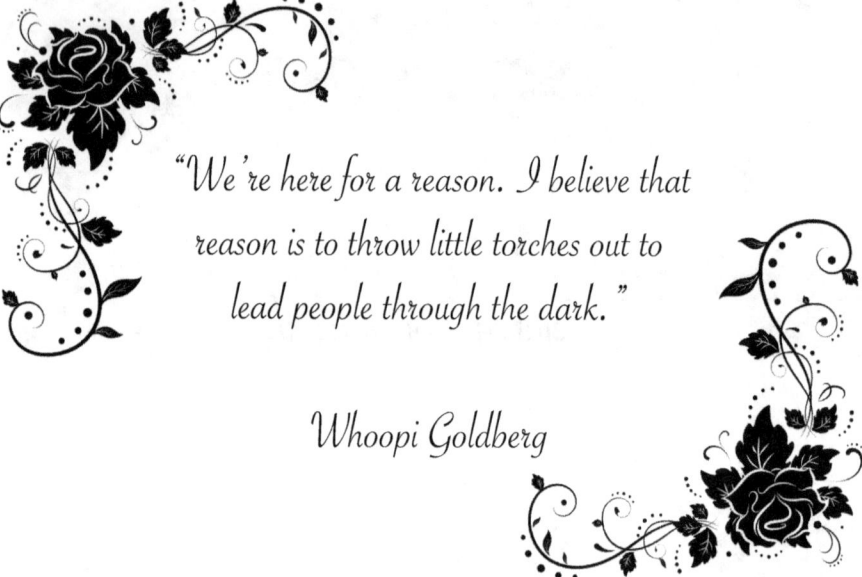

"We're here for a reason. I believe that reason is to throw little torches out to lead people through the dark."

Whoopi Goldberg

"(S)leep gives us a chance to refocus on the essence of who we are. And in that place of connection, it is easier for the fears and concerns of the world to drop away"
Arianna Huffington

SLEEP WELL

Our Rejuvenation Health

WHAT I'VE LEARNED ABOUT SLEEPING WELL

I was used to think sleep was optional. Until the day I crashed.

A few years ago, "busy" was my first, middle and last name. And I was proud of it.

The jobs I took on were habitually hectic, or I made them so by signing up for as many challenges as I could. I stayed late though I was never paid for the extra time. All I wanted was to prove to my bosses and myself what a good employee I was.

I also had commitments outside work, all of which I took seriously. At one point I was studying for a second degree, learning martial arts, volunteering at a nonprofit, and traveling, all around the same time. I refused to sit still. My mantra was "I'll sleep when I'm dead."

MY EXPERIENCE

It took a ground-shaking event for me to realize that lifestyle could kill me.

By then, I'd begun to feel exhausted. I'd gained weight, got sick frequently, and let my temper get the best of me. I was constantly groggy, impatient, frustrated and irritable. It was in the middle of this that tragedy struck.

One fateful night, someone near and dear to me met with a horrible accident and ended up in the emergency room. I remember rushing after the ambulance to the hospital to be told he was in a coma. I'll never forget how I stood still next to the emergency ward, stunned. No one, not even the best physician in the region, could say if this man, who was built like an ox, would live.

I stayed by his bedside for days, feeling like someone had reached inside me and wrung my heart dry. I'd never felt so scared in my life. But I was in such bad condition I couldn't think straight or give the proper care and understanding he needed to recover. I had completely burned out. At the worst time.

That experience taught me how vulnerable we humans are and how precious our lives are. I also recognized that being busy is not what life is all about, that there is so much more to living than what I'd run after until then.

That ordeal opened my eyes to how unprepared I was to deal with a crisis. It made me realize I must take care of myself before I can help others.

MY LESSON

While my loved one recovered quickly and bounced back to normal, my own mindset had changed irrevocably.

It was at this time, one of my girlfriends was diagnosed with breast cancer. Everyone rallied around to support her and her family, from offering to babysit to bringing soup to the hospital. When I asked how I could contribute, she asked me to research breast cancer, its potential causes, healing regimens and how she could get healthy again quickly. I jumped on the task and shared everything I found with her, but I didn't stop even after she recovered.

I kept investigating for four more years. Every extra moment I had, I spent reading, watching, and learning about the health of our body, mind, and spirit. I watched documentaries and listened to talks, interviews, and podcasts by health experts, nutritionists, and physicians. I read article after article from reputable sources and went to health-related seminars whenever I could.

I quickly learned there were many parts of my own life I needed to adjust. I had to improve what I ate, how I exercised, how well I slept, the people I hung out with and the environment I worked in. I also realized that from all these ideas, the fastest and easiest upgrade I could make was to get better sleep.

If I had to make only one change, I thought, I can do that.

IMPORTANCE OF SLEEP

Sleep is what our minds and bodies need so we can be at our optimum during the day. Sleep allows our brains to rejuvenate and our bodies to recuperate and is one of the most important aspects of healthy living.

Though I used to believe I'd catch up on sleep after I died, I realized there was all this living to do before death arrived. And I still had a lot of living left to do.

The accident of my loved one and my friend's cancer cleared the smog from my eyes. It showed me I have only one life to live and that my time on earth is limited.

If I didn't spend this short time I had with joy and in good health, what kind of a life would that be?

Within a week of practicing good sleep habits, I felt better. I stopped feeling exhausted and empty. My irritability and frustrations over petty things lessened. My memory and the quality of my work improved over time.

Most importantly, creating this one habit taught me I could change the other facets of my life. This was the first step in a journey to healing all the areas of myself.

If you, like I was, are feeling overwhelmed with tackling all the areas of your life, start with your sleeping habit first. The benefits are immeasurable and the change is not that difficult. Plus, you'll see results quickly.

It's a perfect place to start.

BENEFITS OF SLEEP

So what are the advantages of getting a good night's rest?

Good sleep:

- Boosts our memory
- Spurs creativity
- Clears our mind and sharpens our thinking
- Helps us learn better and faster
- Improves our mood
- Lowers our stress levels
- Strengthens our immune system
- Reduces the risk of depression
- Enhances stamina
- Manages our weight
- Improves our sex drive
- Curtails injury and sickness
- Avoids accidents
- Curbs inflammation that leads to chronic diseases like cancer and diabetes

Sleep is not a luxury. It's a necessity for our mental and physical well-being.

If you think getting your sleep is being self-indulgent—which so many busy moms and career women say—remember that when you get a full rest at night, you're better equipped to deal with your day, whatever challenges it brings.

When you're at your best, you become a better employee, manager, mother, engineer, teacher, senator, businesswoman or whatever you do. Don't wait for a life-changing event like mine to realize this simple fact.

If sleep is important to you, flip to the next page and answer four key questions on your rejuvenation health. Then, turn to the next part which will give you ten tips on how to incorporate good sleeping habits into your life.

THE STATE OF MY SLEEP HEALTH TODAY

First, four key stock-taking questions.

1. How are you doing in this pillar of your life right now?

- ○ Great! I'm Super Woman at this.
- ○ Okay. I know things can be better but it's not too bad.
- ○ Not too well. I wish things were different.
- ○ Meh. I'm not at all interested in this area.

2. Why is this area of your life important to you right now?

3. Who around you will get inspired when you start taking care of this part of your life?

4. What is your one main goal for enhancing your sleep health this year?

We'll talk about specific tips and actions you can take on the next page, but for now, set an overarching goal for this area of your life for this year.

"The best bridge between despair and hope is a good night's sleep."
E. Joseph Cossman

MY SLEEP HEALTH

TEN TIPS

1. STICK TO A SCHEDULE

Make your bedtime a daily habit. This means going to sleep at the same time every day—yes, even on weekends.
Being consistent with your sleep regulates your internal circadian clock, which will help you fall asleep faster and stay sound asleep longer.

Here's what worked for me. I created a nonnegotiable evening ritual. This is my sacred time, and regardless of how the day went or what's going on around me, it grounds me.

First, I made a conscious decision to get seven and a half hours of sleep no matter what. Then, I scheduled it into my calendar and set an alarm on my phone an hour and a half before bedtime. When the alarm goes off, a pop-up flashes that says, "Take a warm shower, read a book and snuggle in bed." I smile to myself every time I see this and look forward to preparing for bedtime.

I didn't always have this pop-up. When I used only the alarm, I'd groan when I heard it go off, snooze it immediately, and turn back to whatever screen I was staring at with bloodshot eyes. This meant yet another late night and subsequently, bad sleep and a grumpy morning. That tiny pop-up did wonders to pull me away from my desk and into my nightly routine.

So, schedule your sleep and the things you plan to do before bedtime. Set triggers to motivate you to start. Discover little tricks to get you in the mood to prepare for a good night's rest.

This may be hard if you're surrounded by distractions, instant messages, kids and people who demand your attention, but remind them and yourself that you're doing this for the sake of your good health.

2. CREATE A RESTFUL ENVIRONMENT

Make your bedroom the perfect place to sleep. Think of this room as dedicated to two delicious activities—sex and sleep, and nothing else.
Choose a quality mattress and bedding and find comfortable pillows to make your bed cozy and enticing.

We sleep better in cooler conditions, so keep your room at twenty degrees Celsius or less, or at the temperature you consider cold enough but not too chilly.

Keep your room dark. Our brains secrete a hormone called melatonin when there's less light around us, which helps us feel sleepy. If you live in an especially brightly lit area, put up dark shades or wear an eye mask if that would help. If noise bothers you at night, use earplugs or a white noise device to reduce disturbances.

Finally, remove all distractions from your room. That includes televisions, tablets, phones, and even your fur babies if you have any. Sorry, but pets, as cute as they are, move around, wake up during the night, and interfere with our sleep. Fido will have to snooze in his own little bed.

3. WIND DOWN SLOWLY

The hour and a half I transition to bedtime starts with a long warm shower. Others swear by a cold shower but a warm one works well for me. I shower at night because I hate going to bed with the day's grime on me. I find it relaxing and it makes me feel like I'm washing away the troubles I faced during the day. Afterward, I get into my pajamas and slip into bed with my journal and a book.

Reading winds me down and puts me in a good mood. And when I'm snuggled in my comfy bed with my soft pillows and a favorite book in my hands, I feel like I'm encased in luxury.

This is the time of day I take stock of everything I'm grateful for.

I've seen firsthand how people live in different parts of the world. I know what it's like to live in a home with no electricity, no plumbing and an outhouse for a toilet. Knowing hundreds of millions of women have a much harsher life than me makes me immensely thankful for my day, despite how challenging it might have been. This one thought of gratitude crosses my mind every single night, washing away my petty worries.

Think about how you'd like to wind down before bedtime. Make it something you look forward to. Even if your day has gone awry, you'll at least have a good night.

4. MANAGE YOUR WORRIES

I was a habitual worrier.

I even tormented myself about things happening at the other end of the planet, so much so that watching the news threw me into a fit of fury. I've learned to channel this anger into the novels I write, but I found that if I put down my emotions in a journal every night, it dramatically reduces my levels of stress.

There was a time when I'd wake up regularly in the middle of the night with some incensed thought spinning in my mind. Sometimes it would be about an unpleasant incident that happened at the office that day and other times it would be about an injustice I saw on the news, neither of which I could control. So, I'd toss and turn in bed for hours, my mind cursing at the world and refusing to let me get my much-needed sleep.

I curtailed this the day I started to keep a journal.

Every night after my warm shower and before I pick a book to read, I take my journal from the bedside table and jot down three things in bullet form: my biggest win for the day, the one thing I'm grateful for, and my progress on the habits I'm tracking. On tough days, I might add whatever was bothering me to get it off my chest.

Journaling for ten minutes every night has enormously improved the quality of my sleep. It's as if I take all the anxieties from my head and shelve them in between the pages of my journal, so I don't have to dwell on them anymore.

If you're an Olympian worrier like me, start journaling. It might help you get the sleep you need.

5. RESPECT THE THREE-HOUR RULE

I once loved to "eat like the trendy Spaniards," or I liked to think. I'd scoff at anyone who'd go to restaurants before nine and think them a lesser sophisticated species (yes, I was that terrible). That was before I discovered the magic of the three-hour rule.

I now have supper at least three hours before sleep. This change—difficult to make at first, but do-able—had multiple benefits. It helped me manage my weight, reduced the constant bloating I used to experience, and made a world of difference in my sleep.

I fall asleep sooner now because I'm not trying to sleep while my stomach's processing my food intake. In the same vein, I don't go to bed feeling hungry, as that can also keep me up at night with a growling tummy.

If I get the munchies after supper now, I snack on nuts, fruits, or my favorite: almond butter spread on a thin slice of apple or toast. That's tasty and so much better for you than ice cream or potato chips.

I've also stopped using caffeine or alcohol close to bedtime. This doesn't mean I won't have a glass of wine with dinner, especially if it's the weekend and I have company, but I try to respect the three-hour rule.

My recommendation is to stay away from stimulants and sugary, fatty, processed foods, especially before bedtime. Give yourself a three-hour window between eating and sleeping so your body is in its ideal state to rest when you go to bed.

You'll wake up fresher and more energized the next morning and be in better physical condition.

6. UNPLUG YOURSELF

The bright blue light from the screens we use—on computers, tablets, phones, or television—interferes with our sleep patterns. It delays the secretion of our sleepy hormones and increases our levels of alertness, leading to bad sleep. This can make us feel tired and groggy the next day.

I stay away from all screens sixty minutes before sleep. Yes, a whole hour. If you feel like shouting, "I barely have enough time in the day, and you want me to give up another hour I don't have?" I have a trick for you.

Here's what I do.

I love reading and every year, I pledge to read at least forty books. But given my schedule, I rarely accomplish this goal. When I started to unplug before bedtime, I realized I had an extra hour I could spend doing something useful. So I bought print books and horde these next to my nightstand. Every night, I read several chapters from a book for at least forty-five minutes. And voila. I kill two birds with one stone (or feed two birds from one hand, as that's so much nicer).

I now get my sleep and as a bonus, hit my annual reading targets too. And every time I read at night, I sleep like a baby.

So, ask yourself. What fun and useful thing can you do with one hour away from your screens before bedtime?

7. REDUCE NAPPING

Napping often and close to bedtime can interfere with sleep, so watch this habit if you're a frequent napper.

For me, the need to nap is a signal to slow down. I get the urge to nap when I'm coming down with something or am absolutely exhausted or stressed out. In lieu of taking a siesta, I ask myself what's going on in my life I need to stop doing so I can get my energy levels back up. Once I fix the bigger problem, the desire to nap goes away.

If you take regular naps, look at how your days are panning out. What's aggravating you right now? Are there unresolved issues you need to address? Are you consumed with worry about something?

If you still need that nap, rearrange your nap time so it doesn't impact your essential nightly sleep. Stick to napping earlier in the day and keep that time as short as possible. Limiting your naps to fifteen to twenty minutes and not napping too close to bedtime will help you get better sleep during the night.

8. GET PHYSICAL

We've all heard this before. Exercising is good for sleep. It's known to lower the risk of insomnia and sleep apnea and in general, give you a higher quality rest at night.

Having a physical workout routine increases the time we spend in the deep sleep stage. This is when our breathing slows down, our heart rate regulates, and our muscles relax, all of which allow our brain and body cells to rejuvenate.

If all you do is go for a walk during your lunch break or take the stairs to your office, that will help. Light activity is better than none. But remember not to exercise too close to bedtime, as that can stimulate you rather than prepare you for sleep.

Other than helping us to sleep better, exercising has many other benefits which we'll go into in Section 3—*Move Well*.

9. DEAL WITH SLEEP PROBLEMS

Have you ever found yourself wide awake at three a.m. staring at the ceiling? I have, many times, especially when I used to work in my former taxing job.

My personal trick to managing insomnia is to prop myself up on my pillows and pick up a nonfiction book. Very soon, my head's nodding over the pages and I'm ready to sink into bed and sleep tight. Novels don't work too well, especially if they're in the thriller/suspense genre. Those have me up till early morning, fighting sleep.

Keep in mind, though, sleep therapists recommend that you leave your bed and go to another room altogether whenever you can't sleep. This way, you don't end up sitting in bed kicking your sheets and getting frustrated. When you leave your bedroom at such times, you stop associating it with feelings of restlessness. It reinforces in your mind that your bed is devoted to sleep and sex.

On that note, if you can't sleep, you could nudge your sweetie awake for a midnight romp if he or she is up for it. It's a great way to relax your mind and body and increase your chances of a good sleep for the remainder of the night.

The important lesson here is not to toss and turn and wish yourself to sleep. Find the tricks that will get you back to sleep or get up and do something else, so you don't aggravate the matter further.

Everyone deals with sleep issues differently. If your issue is severe, you may need to visit your physician and get professional help.

10. KEEP A SLEEP DIARY

If you have trouble with your sleep often or if you find your sleep patterns are irregular, keep a record of how you prepare for bedtime and how well you sleep at night.

Write down the stresses you encountered on those days you have a hard time sleeping. Think about what you ate for supper and when. Ask yourself if what you're engaged in right before bedtime is helping or hindering your sleep. Do this for four weeks and you'll see patterns emerge.

You may decipher the problem and come up with solutions yourself. If the issue persists, your physician can make a proper diagnosis, and taking your nightly record to them will help them solve your problem more quickly.

THE HABIT MAKER

Let's Make These Stick

Pick one idea from the tips list and try it out for one month. Do this for thirty days and see how you do. Then, if you can, try a new one next month.

So, what is *one* action you'll take to incorporate sleep fitness into your life this month?

Go back to the annual goal you set at the start of this section and make sure the activity you choose links to your goals.

Set January Activity:
Track the Activity: Check back at the end of the month to see how well you did
○ Great! I was Super Woman at this.   ○ Good. I managed this most of the time.   ○ Okay, I guess. I know I can get better.   ○ Not so well. So, maybe I need to try this again. Who said you have to get it right the first time.
How can I improve next month?

Set February Activity:

Track the Activity: Check back at the end of the month to see how well you did

- ○ Great! I was Super Woman at this.
- ○ Good. I managed this most of the time.
- ○ Okay, I guess. I know I can get better.
- ○ Not so well. So, maybe I need to try this again. Who said you have to get it right the first time.

How can I improve next month?

Set March Activity:

Track the Activity: Check back at the end of the month to see how well you did

- ○ Great! I was Super Woman at this.
- ○ Good. I managed this most of the time.
- ○ Okay, I guess. I know I can get better.
- ○ Not so well. So, maybe I need to try this again. Who said you have to get it right the first time.

How can I improve next month?

Set April Activity:

Track the Activity: Check back at the end of the month to see how well you did

- ○ Great! I was Super Woman at this.
- ○ Good. I managed this most of the time.
- ○ Okay, I guess. I know I can get better.
- ○ Not so well. So, maybe I need to try this again. Who said you have to get it right the first time.

How can I improve next month?

Set May Activity:

Track the Activity: Check back at the end of the month to see how well you did

- ○ Great! I was Super Woman at this.
- ○ Good. I managed this most of the time.
- ○ Okay, I guess. I know I can get better.
- ○ Not so well. So, maybe I need to try this again. Who said you have to get it right the first time.

How can I improve next month?

Set June Activity:

Track the Activity: Check back at the end of the month to see how well you did

- ○ Great! I was Super Woman at this.
- ○ Good. I managed this most of the time.
- ○ Okay, I guess. I know I can get better.
- ○ Not so well. So, maybe I need to try this again. Who said you have to get it right the first time.

How can I improve next month?

Set July Activity:

Track the Activity: Check back at the end of the month to see how well you did

- ○ Great! I was Super Woman at this.
- ○ Good. I managed this most of the time.
- ○ Okay, I guess. I know I can get better.
- ○ Not so well. So, maybe I need to try this again. Who said you have to get it right the first time.

How can I improve next month?

Set August Activity:

Track the Activity: Check back at the end of the month to see how well you did

- ○ Great! I was Super Woman at this.
- ○ Good. I managed this most of the time.
- ○ Okay, I guess. I know I can get better.
- ○ Not so well. So, maybe I need to try this again. Who said you have to get it right the first time.

How can I improve next month?

Set September Activity:

Track the Activity: Check back at the end of the month to see how well you did

- ○ Great! I was Super Woman at this.
- ○ Good. I managed this most of the time.
- ○ Okay, I guess. I know I can get better.
- ○ Not so well. So, maybe I need to try this again. Who said you have to get it right the first time.

How can I improve next month?

Set October Activity:

Track the Activity: Check back at the end of the month to see how well you did

- ○ Great! I was Super Woman at this.
- ○ Good. I managed this most of the time.
- ○ Okay, I guess. I know I can get better.
- ○ Not so well. So, maybe I need to try this again. Who said you have to get it right the first time.

How can I improve next month?

Set November Activity:

Track the Activity: Check back at the end of the month to see how well you did

- ○ Great! I was Super Woman at this.
- ○ Good. I managed this most of the time.
- ○ Okay, I guess. I know I can get better.
- ○ Not so well. So, maybe I need to try this again. Who said you have to get it right the first time.

How can I improve next month?

Set December Activity:

Track the Activity: Check back at the end of the month to see how well you did
O Great! I was Super Woman at this. O Good. I managed this most of the time. O Okay, I guess. I know I can get better. O Not so well. So, maybe I need to try this again. Who said you have to get it right the first time.
How can I improve next month?

SO, HOW DO YOU FEEL?

That's the end of this section. What do you think of the answers you gave here? If something wasn't captured in this section but you want to get it out of your system, this is the place to do so.

Your Rebel Life

SECTION THREE
MOVE WELL

Physical Health

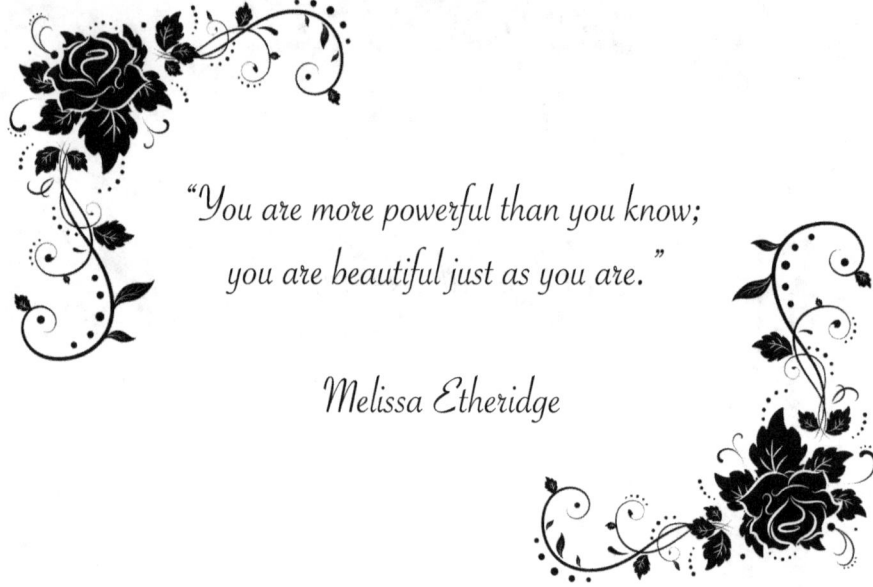

"You are more powerful than you know; you are beautiful just as you are."

Melissa Etheridge

"Take care of your body. It's the only place you have to live."
Jim Rohn

MOVE WELL

Our Physical Health

WHAT I'VE LEARNED ABOUT MOVING WELL

How do you perceive your body?

I'm not asking if you think you're too fat/too skinny, too short/too tall, or too dark/too fair. The question I'm asking is why do you think your body exists? A strange thought I know, but the answer you give to this simple query will determine your physical health.

So, how do you perceive your body?

Answer here:

THE MIRACLE OF OUR BODIES

My body, as I see it, is a vessel which carries me for the duration of my life on Earth.

Before you think I'm getting all woo-woo on you, let me explain.

Comparable to a plane, a car, or a motorcycle we'd use to travel from one end of the country to the other, we need a vehicle to get from birth to death on our journey in life. The state of that vehicle and how we treat it during the trek will decide how comfortable and enjoyable our trip will be. This is true for a car we drive across the country or the bodies in which we live till our last breath.

Before we go on a major road trip, we may service our car, check the tires, and make sure the tank is full. As we roll through the roads, we'll continue to fill that tank up, ensure tire pressure is at its optimum, and try not to bang the doors on concrete posts on strange streets. If we own that car, we will be extra careful how we handle it or how we let others treat it.

Sadly though, many people look after their cars better than their own bodies. This is because they don't understand the value of their physical bodies and the incredible feats our bodies are capable of. They don't perceive the important role our bodies play in getting us through life.

Yes, there are brave souls who have created successful lives despite not having all their limbs or even organs intact. Look at Kyle Menard, who was the first quadruple amputee to climb Mount Kilimanjaro with no support or prosthetics. His attitude and gumption make him a modern-day superhero, an incredibly inspiring human being.

But for most of us, there's not a lot we can accomplish without a wholesome, healthy body. Our bodies allow us to do everything in life, from breathing to walking to laughing and much, much more. Yet, we take them for granted.

But if we stop to think about it, our human bodies are phenomenal organic machines.

Our hearts beat, on average, between sixty to a hundred times per minute and pump 2,000 gallons of blood a day. Our blood travels twelve thousand miles a day, equivalent to four cross-country trips in the US. A trillion nerves power our memory and nerve impulses from the brain can travel at a speed of 274 kilometers an hour, almost as fast as a bullet train. To rejuvenate itself, our skin sheds 500 million cells a day and continue replenishing itself daily. Our body does all this and more without us having to even blink an eye.

Our precious organs, from our beating hearts to our life-affirming lungs to our astoundingly amazing brains, need to continue to work as they should. For all this to happen, we need to service our bodies like we service our cars, even if it's for as little as a few minutes a day.

A cross-country road trip can take a few days, but our personal life journey can last up to eighty, ninety or a hundred years if we're lucky. If we desire to travel in a happy and blissful state through our time on this planet, we'd better start taking care of ourselves.

So, let's show some respect to these marvelous bodies of ours.

A MINDSET SHIFT

Some of you are going to hate hearing this.

Before we start nitpicking on pimples, bad tan lines, or horrible lipstick colors, we must appreciate our bodies for the miracle machines they are. Pay less attention to the color of your nails and the wrinkles around your eyes and focus on the strength of your heart for a change.

This means we must work out regularly. Find an exercise regimen that fits you and follow it consistently on a daily or at least, weekly basis. Instead of spending two hours at the hairdresser or the nail spa every Saturday, use that time to move your body.

I realize this may sound harsh, and I also understand this is your body we're talking about. You get to choose what to prioritize, but remember that decision will determine your physical health for the rest of your life.

OUR CURRENT STATE

Physical exercise is on the decline globally as more and more people live more sedentary lives.

A recent study by the World Health Organization (WHO) showed that almost three million deaths every year can be attributed to being sedentary. Inactivity and obesity are linked to a myriad of ailments like heart disease, diabetes, colon cancer, high blood pressure, osteoporosis, depression, anxiety, insomnia, loss of libido, and as the WHO study determined, even premature death.

More people around the world die from being overweight than from being underweight today. Sobering facts.

And, sitting is the new smoking. In North America alone, adults watch at least four hours of television a day and the rest of the world is catching up. But how much damage are we doing to our bodies from excessive television watching, social media engagement, and long commutes to work?

PHYSICAL FITNESS

Let's turn this conversation around and find out what the benefits of getting physically fit are.

An active lifestyle:

- Reduces the risk of chronic illnesses such as cancer, diabetes, high blood pressure, heart disease, stroke, and depression, among others.
- Helps you sleep better, which allows your brain to regenerate and be more alert and productive during the day.
- Helps you support a healthy weight suited to your body and avoid obesity, which can lead to chronic illnesses, depression, and other debilitating ailments.
- Builds stronger muscles, bones, and joints, which reduces the risk of arthritis and pain from falls.
- Strengthens your immune system and reduces your risk of getting sick.
- Improves your mood and mental well-being, which reduces your risk of depression.
- Improves long-term memory and stops your brain functions from declining as you grow older.

- Improves the look and feel of your skin and keeps you looking young.
- Increases your confidence level and makes you feel better about yourself.
- Increase your chances of living longer.

Why wouldn't you want to take care of your body?

OUR OPTIONS

Most experts recommend at least thirty minutes of moderately intense exercise every day.

This isn't complicated, and you have many options. You can garden, take a walk during lunch, play a game of baseball after work, or go for a hike in the woods every weekend. You can even add household chores to your regular physical routine. The most important thing is to choose activities you enjoy doing. This way, it will be easy to start, and you'll have less friction in making it a habit.

So what moderate exercises can you choose from?

- Dancing
- Golfing
- Going for a brisk walk
- Gardening and mowing the lawn
- Biking at a leisurely pace
- Hiking at a leisurely pace
- Swimming at a leisurely pace
- Canoeing at a leisurely pace
- And much more…

If you want to take it to the next level, try your hand at more vigorous activities like running, bicycling, aerobics, swimming laps, hiking uphill, and competitive sports like football, hockey, tennis, and much, much more.

BODY IMAGE

Before we go further, there's one misconception I'd like to clarify.

Having a healthy and fit body does not equal being skinny. Not by a long mile.

Staying fit means maintaining a body that functions the way it's designed to and keeps you in optimal health.

You see, body image and beauty are social constructs and thus relative, depending on where in the world you live.

When I was growing up in East Africa, some of my traditionally built buxom teachers would pinch my cheek, and tsk to say, "This girl needs more meat on her. How will she ever find a husband being so skinny like this?" Or they'd shake their heads and say with concern in their eyes, "Doesn't your family feed you, little girl?" I spent my entire adolescence obsessing over why my hips and boobs wouldn't grow fuller so I could look like the other beautiful girls in school.

Then, when I arrived in North America, my college frenemies would say with not-so-friendly looks, "Must be nice to be skinny. Why do you even work out? Tryna get skinnier and make us look bad?" That began a few confused years when I tried to stay as skinny as I possibly could to adapt to this new body image thrust on me.

Why do we succumb to these artificial imaginings of what beauty is?

We all know the impact of popular media on our body image, especially for us women. Magazines, television, social media, and advertising from the beauty industry bombard us with images of an "ideal" beauty standard.

But, we're all different. We're built with different body types, bone structures, and metabolic rates. Given the variations in our ages, genetics, health histories, number of pregnancies, and the work we do, it's impossible to compare ourselves to anyone or anything other than the health markers applicable to us and us alone.

HOW TO MEASURE

I don't own a weighing scale or subscribe to "beauty" magazines anymore. I focus my energy on sustaining a healthy lifestyle and do annual physical and dental checkups to confirm my health status.

Every spring, my family doctor and my dentist carry out checkups, including X-rays, blood tests, and Pap tests where warranted and give me a verdict. From my doctor, I get my cholesterol levels, red blood cell counts, and a calculation of my body mass index in a comprehensive health report. From my dentist, I get a check on my cavities and gums and get X-rays every few years to identify hidden issues.

If I'm within the normal healthy range for my body type, I continue doing what I'm doing. If not, I make the dietary or fitness adjustments they recommend. Working toward annual report cards from health experts has stopped me from trying to attain an elusive weight goal or doing anything unhealthy for short-term gains.

I'm happy to spend my hard-earned money on insurance that gives me access to these key services, rather than spending it on expensive diets that hardly work or on fighting potential debilitating illnesses in the future.

Love your beautiful body for what it is. It's all we have to take us through this life. Let's give it the respect and care it deserves.

Focus on your health. Everything else is secondary.

In the next chapter, you'll get ten tips on how to improve the health of your physical state.

You don't have to adopt all of them. Try out one new habit every month. If you pursue even a fifth of these techniques, you'll feel fitter, healthier and happier than a majority of the people around you.

THE STATE OF MY PHYSICAL HEALTH TODAY

First, four key stock-taking questions.

1. How are you doing in this pillar of your life right now?

- ○ Great! I'm Super Woman at this.
- ○ Okay. I know things can be better but it's not too bad.
- ○ Not too well. I wish things were different.
- ○ Meh. I'm not at all interested in this area.

2. Why is this area of your life important to you right now?

3. Who around you will get inspired when you start taking care of this part of your life?

4. What is your one main goal for enhancing your physical health this year?

We'll talk about specific tips and actions you can take on the next page, but for now, set an overarching goal for this area of your life for this year.

"Movement is a medicine for creating change in a person's physical, emotional, and mental states."
Carol Welch

MY PHYSICAL HEALTH

TEN TIPS

1. FIND YOUR WHY

As with anything, start with your why.

Ask yourself why you want to adopt a regular exercise regime. Is it to improve your health? To look sexier? To live longer? Feel more confident?

My trigger was seeing the corrosive impact of unhealthy lifestyle decisions on my friends, family, and colleagues. They were all smart, educated folk, but they were too busy or overworked for self-care, or they focused more on their looks than their health and the results showed up when they hit their forties. One by one, they ended up with various sicknesses of their own making.

Then, having a loved one in a hospital for a month exposed me to the health care system of a first-world country with a supposedly "world-class health policy." The system worked like a huge conveyor belt filled with sick people who were medicated more often than mended. It was a cold and unsympathetic machine that had no care for the feelings of people who were at their most vulnerable. That experience was an eye-opener.

My motivation to get on the workout mat every morning is to never end up in the clutches of that "health care" system. I don't want to see the inside of another hospital for the rest of my life if I can help it.

What are your reasons for wanting a healthy body?

If your motivation is compelling enough, you'll keep this habit in the long-term.

2. SET AND TRACK GOALS

The most effective way to develop a fitness regimen is to set goals and track your progress.

Figure out what you want to do by the end of the year, then work backward. Break your goal down into months or quarters (every three months). Focus on your health outcomes and not solely on your weight.

I'm a nerdy writer with not a bone of athleticism in my body. So when I initially, and overambitiously, set a goal to work out one hour every day, I got so overwhelmed, I almost quit. Instead of giving up, I broke my goal down into four parts: yoga warm-up, strength, cardio, and a yoga cooldown. Then, I gave myself a year to build each piece into my morning routine. Yes, a full year.

After I planned this out, I walked into a neighborhood gym and asked a personal trainer to go over my idea. Using her advice, I refined the plan, removing exercises she said wouldn't help and adding those she recommended.

The next day, I started with a five-minute yoga warm-up, promising myself that I'd add the next pieces one by one in five-minute blocks. Five minutes was all it took to begin. It was hard to say no to such a short practice. It made me feel silly not to start.

Then, every night I journaled what I did so I could track my progress.

I wrote down how many minutes I worked out that day and put a happy face and a gold star next to any bullet that said something like, "I did one extra push up today!!!" What motivated me in kindergarten seems to work for me as an adult too.

Setting an annual goal, creating an incremental plan, tracking it every day and acknowledging my wins did wonders to create a habit I first thought was impossible.

There will be space for you to write down your fitness goals in the next part of this chapter, but start thinking about your annual objectives now.

What do you want to achieve in physical fitness a year from now? How could you break that goal down into practical chunks? How will you track your progress? Let these questions percolate in your brain as you go through the remaining tips.

3. DO IT FIRST THING

By getting my physical training done and out of the way as soon as I wake up, I can tick off one important accomplishment in my journal at night. That makes me feel good even if the rest of the day had gone to hell in a handbasket.

But here's the main reason I work out in the morning: it's because there are fewer people to interrupt me, and there are fewer excuses I can give myself.

Incorporating exercises into my morning ritual also sends a strong signal to myself that this is an essential part of my day. Making it part of a "ritual" means this is serious. It isn't ad hoc or something I do when I feel like it. *This is my ritual!* I keep telling myself on those days I feel like skipping.

There are many good reasons for doing your workout first thing in the morning, but here's the best I've heard, from exercise guru Marsha Doble. She says, "I have to exercise in the morning before my brain figures out what I'm doing." Sometimes it pays to play mind games with ourselves.

Find the best time in the morning to incorporate your physical fitness activities. Make sure it's a time when there are fewer distractions and demands on you. Then, do it!

4. SCHEDULE YOUR ROUTINE

It sounds counterintuitive, but scheduling your exercise routine is freeing. It gets done—making you the boss of your day rather than the other way around.

It's great to have fitness goals, but the most effective way to accomplish them is to schedule them in a calendar. I'm a heavy user of my online calendar and have learned that when I plan my days and weeks and write my priorities down next to a timeline, I achieve my objectives without having to overthink any of it.

Schedule your exercises into your calendar, whether it's online or on paper. Add a happy face or a gold star every time you exercise to give you a mini incentive to stick with your plans.

5. SET YOURSELF UP FOR SUCCESS

Some days, I swear there's a little green devil crouching on my shoulder, urging me to skip my routine "just for today." It's tempting to listen to it, so I've found a trick to make it easier for me to start every morning.

I prepare my training gear the night before. I install my yoga mat outside my bedroom so I stumble onto it as soon as I leave the room, reminding me of what I need to do next. I also put my gym clothes right next to my towel in the bathroom, so as soon as I wash my face, I can reach for them without even opening my eyes.

The less friction, the better.

This is also why I work out at home rather than outside or at the local gym. I've found that going to the gym gives too many opportunities for that little green devil to settle comfortably on my shoulders and make me say "maybe not today." Putting my gym shoes on, picking up my car keys, heading down to the garage, and driving to the gym all require extra motivation and momentum, so I cut it all out.

I have no excuse when the mat is already rolled out. All I have to do is get on it and start stretching, even if it means all I have on are my bra and panties. Then, that little green devil falls off my shoulders instantly. It's easy, uncomplicated, and once it becomes a habit, it's hard to imagine starting my day any other way.

So, ask yourself this. How can you prepare your environment so you don't have to think too hard to start?

6. FIND A MOTIVATOR

Make your workout fun.

You can do this with a music playlist that inspires you, an accountability partner who cheers you on, or a personal trainer who encourages you.

Since I do my exercises early in the morning at home, I have to galvanize myself. I created a yoga music playlist to get me going and follow it with a series of motivational videos for the core and cardio portion of my training.

Sometimes that little green devil reappears on my shoulder to whisper gawd-do-you-really-wanna-do-lunges-today? But when one of my virtual mentors—Mel Robbins, Marie Forleo, Eric Thomas, Brendon Burchard, Les Brown, or Tony Robbins among others—is talking about their successes, their sacrifices, and how they never quit, it's easy to do one more lunge or one more sit-up. It's embarrassing not to.

I now look forward to my morning routine. I jump out of bed, wondering who has a new video out and what interesting life lesson I'll learn that day.

Finding little tricks like this will encourage you to do what you must do.

What would motivate you to start and finish your exercise routine? Prepare this in advance so you're not fiddling with it in the morning. Don't give yourself any excuses not to start.

7. MOVE EVERY DAY

You may not have time for a daily exercise routine, especially if your schedule is erratic or your needs get overtaken by other people's (bosses, spouses, children…) demands. But any movement at any time of the day is beneficial.

If you're going a few flights up, take the stairs instead of the elevator. Park your car at the end of the lot (in a well-lit, safe spot) and walk to your building. Take a short hike during your lunch hour rather than sit at your desk or in the cafeteria. Have your soup and sandwich, then get out and go for a jog at a nearby park, or at least a stroll around the block.

Active breaks like these will keep your body healthy and your mind clear. And you'll become more productive when you return to work.

Over the years, I've taught myself to take the stairs whenever I need to go up four floors or fewer. This habit is so ingrained in me now that I feel put off when the stairway isn't accessible or I'm forced to use the elevator. Four floors are my max for now, and I get a kick out of running to the top, while my bigger and younger male colleagues huff and puff their way behind me.

Look for everyday experiences and turn them into your exercise routine. Make your activities a game and have fun with them.

8. WATCH YOUR POSTURE

We must be aware of how we hold our bodies, especially if we stick to only one activity for most of the day. Standing all day long is as bad as sitting all day long.

Maintaining correct posture will keep your spine and bones in alignment, help your muscles move properly, and reduce stress on your ligaments. It can mitigate future health issues like arthritis and tension headaches even.

To avoid these problems, schedule regular breaks and move or stretch in between long periods of doing one activity. Alternate between sitting and standing so your body's in motion most of the time.

If you can afford it, get an ergonomic assessment and find out what desk, chair, keyboard, telephone headset or other equipment is most appropriate for you. If you're feeling adventurous, use a trampoline or treadmill desk or get a plain old stand-up desk which goes for a hundred dollars or less these days.

These adjustments can reduce a lifetime of back pain, muscle pain, eye strain, and headaches. Take your posture seriously, starting now.

9. LISTEN TO YOUR BODY

Our bodies are great at sending signals when things aren't right with us.

Listen to your body and recognize the signs when you're not well. When this happens, take the necessary steps to get back to normal as quickly as you can. As soon as you feel you're not one hundred percent, get more rest, eat better, move more, or take the vitamins or supplements your body may need.

Many busy people become ill because they ignore early warning signs, only to get laid up for weeks. I used to think my life was too hectic to take time off when I got sick, but this made things worse. It put me out for longer than if I'd taken care of myself from the start.

Another reason to stay home and take care of yourself is to stop contagions. This is a common courtesy we can give our colleagues, and they'll appreciate us for it. Coming to work when you're sick is distressing for your health and that of your coworkers' as well.

10. GET REGULAR CHECKUPS

Not everyone lives in a place where medical and dental care is easily accessible or affordable. If you are lucky to have this opportunity, take advantage of it and make appointments for your annual checkups today.

If you're concerned about expenses, think about the physical, emotional and financial toll you're lightening by paying up-front to prevent chronic illnesses. I cut television and cable from my life and funnel that money toward my health insurance. If it's important to you, you'll find a way.

If you think this is an impossible goal, consider this: if you cut TV altogether, you'll save more than $1,500 annually, and if you stop buying that daily boutique (and unhealthy) frappuccino, you can rustle up another $1,500 a year. That's a great start!

There are no guarantees. But, sticking to a healthy lifestyle and getting yourself checked regularly, will drastically curtail your probability of getting sick. Call the nearest clinic, confirm your appointment, and put the date on your calendar as a recurring annual event. Do this for yourself and your family.

In between your annual appointments, eat well, sleep well, move well, and surround yourself with positive and encouraging people.

THE HABIT MAKER

Let's Make These Stick

Pick one idea from the tips list and try it out for one month. Do this for thirty days and see how you do. Then, if you can, try a new one next month.

So, what is *one* action you'll take to incorporate physical fitness into your life this month?

Go back to the annual goal you set at the start of this section and make sure the activity you choose links to your goals.

Set January Activity:
Track the Activity: Check back at the end of the month to see how well you did
○ Great! I was Super Woman at this. ○ Good. I managed this most of the time. ○ Okay, I guess. I know I can get better. ○ Not so well. So, maybe I need to try this again. Who said you have to get it right the first time.
How can I improve next month?

Set February Activity:

Track the Activity: Check back at the end of the month to see how well you did

- ○ Great! I was Super Woman at this.
- ○ Good. I managed this most of the time.
- ○ Okay, I guess. I know I can get better.
- ○ Not so well. So, maybe I need to try this again. Who said you have to get it right the first time.

How can I improve next month?

Set March Activity:

Track the Activity: Check back at the end of the month to see how well you did

- ○ Great! I was Super Woman at this.
- ○ Good. I managed this most of the time.
- ○ Okay, I guess. I know I can get better.
- ○ Not so well. So, maybe I need to try this again. Who said you have to get it right the first time.

How can I improve next month?

Set April Activity:

Track the Activity: Check back at the end of the month to see how well you did

- ○ Great! I was Super Woman at this.
- ○ Good. I managed this most of the time.
- ○ Okay, I guess. I know I can get better.
- ○ Not so well. So, maybe I need to try this again. Who said you have to get it right the first time.

How can I improve next month?

Set May Activity:

Track the Activity: Check back at the end of the month to see how well you did

- ○ Great! I was Super Woman at this.
- ○ Good. I managed this most of the time.
- ○ Okay, I guess. I know I can get better.
- ○ Not so well. So, maybe I need to try this again. Who said you have to get it right the first time.

How can I improve next month?

Set June Activity:

Track the Activity: Check back at the end of the month to see how well you did

- ○ Great! I was Super Woman at this.
- ○ Good. I managed this most of the time.
- ○ Okay, I guess. I know I can get better.
- ○ Not so well. So, maybe I need to try this again. Who said you have to get it right the first time.

How can I improve next month?

Set July Activity:

Track the Activity: Check back at the end of the month to see how well you did

- ○ Great! I was Super Woman at this.
- ○ Good. I managed this most of the time.
- ○ Okay, I guess. I know I can get better.
- ○ Not so well. So, maybe I need to try this again. Who said you have to get it right the first time.

How can I improve next month?

Set August Activity:

Track the Activity: Check back at the end of the month to see how well you did
○ Great! I was Super Woman at this. ○ Good. I managed this most of the time. ○ Okay, I guess. I know I can get better. ○ Not so well. So, maybe I need to try this again. Who said you have to get it right the first time.
How can I improve next month?

Set September Activity:

Track the Activity: Check back at the end of the month to see how well you did
○ Great! I was Super Woman at this. ○ Good. I managed this most of the time. ○ Okay, I guess. I know I can get better. ○ Not so well. So, maybe I need to try this again. Who said you have to get it right the first time.
How can I improve next month?

Set October Activity:

Track the Activity: Check back at the end of the month to see how well you did
○ Great! I was Super Woman at this. ○ Good. I managed this most of the time. ○ Okay, I guess. I know I can get better. ○ Not so well. So, maybe I need to try this again. Who said you have to get it right the first time.
How can I improve next month?

Set November Activity:

Track the Activity: Check back at the end of the month to see how well you did
○ Great! I was Super Woman at this. ○ Good. I managed this most of the time. ○ Okay, I guess. I know I can get better. ○ Not so well. So, maybe I need to try this again. Who said you have to get it right the first time.
How can I improve next month?

Your Rebel Life

Set December Activity:
Track the Activity: Check back at the end of the month to see how well you did
○ Great! I was Super Woman at this. ○ Good. I managed this most of the time. ○ Okay, I guess. I know I can get better. ○ Not so well. So, maybe I need to try this again. Who said you have to get it right the first time.
How can I improve next month?

SO, HOW DO YOU FEEL?

That's the end of this section. What do you think of the answers you gave here? If something wasn't captured in this section but you want to get it out of your system, this is the place to do so.

Your Rebel Life

SECTION FOUR
EAT WELL

Nutrition Health

"Everyone has inside of her a piece of good news. The good news is that you don't know how great you can be, how much you can love, what you can accomplish, and what your potential is."

Anne Frank

> *"The food you eat can be either the safest and most powerful form of medicine or the slowest form of poison."*
> *Ann Wigmore*

EAT WELL

Our Nutrition Health

Caution: This section is not for everyone. If you feel furious at the mere mention of healthy foods, have no desire to eat healthy or believe there's a global conspiracy at play to force you to eat better, *please* skip this section. This is only for those who are open to learning about the myths of foods and eating habits.

WHAT I'VE LEARNED ABOUT EATING WELL

If you want one good reason to eat healthy, it's this: Eating well reduces your risk of contracting the worst chronic illnesses of the twenty-first century.

I know what you're thinking. *I thought we were done with this depressing stuff. Didn't we cover this in the last section?*

The facts are: if we don't sleep well, we get sick. If we don't move well, we get sick. If we don't eat well, we get sick. We must take care of all these areas, or we won't get through this life in good condition.

If you're tired of hearing gory stats, scroll down (or flip the page if you're reading this in print) and get to the tips in the next part. Stay on if you'd like to bust the myths of healthy eating.

THE GORY STATS

You're still here? Thanks for sticking with me for the rest of this. I promise to keep this short. Well, short…ish.

Here are the lurid facts. Diabetes and high blood pressure are on the rise. Dementia, Alzheimer's, and other cognitive degenerative diseases are increasing everywhere. Heart attacks, strokes, and cancer have become a global phenomena.

Smoking, excessive drinking and being sedentary trigger these diseases, but what we put into our body three times a day or more has a bigger impact on our health. Our societies are getting sicker because we're choosing the wrong foods and we're eating too much of them.

A 2016 global study by the World Health Organization (WHO) showed obesity growing in alarming numbers. Almost forty percent of adults and eighteen percent of children aged five to nineteen are considered overweight. As many as forty-one million children under five worldwide are overweight or obese. If current trends continue, seventy percent of adults will soon be predisposed to type two diabetes, heart disease, stroke, cancer, and other such illnesses.

Seventy percent of the world! Think of that.

This is a global pandemic that takes lives and costs billions of dollars in health care. These are staggering and distressing numbers, especially when scientists say this epidemic is preventable. Yes, you heard right. Being overweight or becoming obese is entirely preventable.

We can sit on our couches and blame our genes. We can point the finger at our parents, the media or the government. External forces and our family history can impact our eating habits, but we have more control over our bodies than we think. It's up to us to make healthy choices.

Nobody force-feeds us or holds a weapon to our heads at breakfast, lunch, and supper. We put food in our mouths willingly using our own two hands. Don't we?

As world renown physician and author of *How Not to Die*, Dr. Michael Greger, likes to say: "Genes may load the gun, but it's lifestyle that pulls the trigger."

Yes, there are food desert neighborhoods where fresh produce is hard to find, but this is not an insurmountable challenge to overcome. And yes, there's no magic switch to change our behavior overnight, but given the enormous health risks we're exposing ourselves to, could we at least make the attempt to shift gears?

Our other option is to roll over and wait for these horrible illnesses to catch up to us, and end up with tragic and shortened lives. And we'll become yet another statistic.

There are so many alternatives available today, with nutritious and diverse foods from around the world becoming available everywhere. There are recipes and cooking ideas galore at our fingertips. Healthy eating is not only an opportunity to feel and look better. It can also be an enjoyable activity.

A FEW MYTHS

Before we move to the juicy tips, let's go over the main myths surrounding nutrition.

Most of these myths are propagated by the very industries that market their products to us. Their messages are tailored to make us feel good about making the wrong choices so we continue to buy what they sell. We love to believe their stories without question because we feel these industries give us (happily so) permission to continue our bad habits.

We love it when others confirm our own biases. It's human nature.

But shouldn't we check where we get our information from, think critically and make up our own minds? Shouldn't we ask the right questions so we don't get caught into unhealthy traps?

There's a reason there are huge lobby groups for the processed, fast-food, meat and dairy industries. When was the last time you heard of The Kale Lobby? Or Big Broccoli? When anyone spends multi-millions, even billions, to sway political decisions, you know they care more for their bottom line than the good health of you and me. Think about it.

Okay, let's tackle some untruths here.

A warning though. Some of you will not want to hear any of this, so read only if you're serious about your health. And, don't take this information as gospel. Do your own research and stay informed. That is the single smartest decision you can make.

Myth 1: Counting calories is the most important thing to do.

The diet industry has capitalized on this for decades.

What's more important than counting calories? It is to understand the type and amount of nutrients in your meals. If you eat food full of vitamins, minerals, complex carbs, proteins, good fats, and fiber, all of which a human body needs to function well, you don't need to count calories.

If you plan your meals around nutrition, you'll automatically reach for foods that won't expand your waistline or harm your heart. Plus, you'll have a plethora of diverse foods to choose from. You don't have to restrict yourself other than to stay away from exorbitantly sugary, fatty, and salty foods. This doesn't have to be complicated.

One trick I use here is to create the most colorful plate I can for every meal. This means a variety of fruits for breakfast and a wonderful array of vegetables for lunch and supper. I get my fill of essential nutrients, plus I enjoy both the preparation and the consumption of my meals.

Instead of agonizing over calories and feeling deprived, why not prepare nutrient-dense meals instead?

Myth 2: We crave certain foods because we're deficient in the nutrients they provide.

This is a myth many of us would love to be true.

So, if we crave a tub of caramel ice cream and a packet of deep-fried chocolate-covered donuts, we're missing nutrients that come from these foods, correct? That would be a nice belief to have, but the fact is ice cream and fried donuts don't have many nutrients if any at all. (Please don't shoot! I'm just the messenger.)

Our cravings come from our taste buds conditioned through years of bad habits that incite us to stuff ourselves with bad fat, salt, or sugar.

For a small group of people, cravings may well arise from a nutritional deficiency. For most of us, though, a hankering for fatty, high-sugar foods is caused by our emotional state. Negative moods, high stress, poor hydration, or lack of sleep can make us covet the bad stuff.

Next time you get a craving for unhealthy junk food, ask yourself if there are other factors behind it.

Myth 3: Detoxifying is good for you.

If you fast for short periods, do it after a proper discussion with your physician. Short-term detoxification fads have no long-term benefits and can even be harmful to your body.

The main reason you'd need to detoxify is because you're ingesting a lot of harmful food, such as highly processed junk foods. Otherwise, why detoxify? Think about it. The most logical thing you can do is to avoid putting these toxins in your body in the first place.

Your body is designed to detoxify naturally. Help your body by eating healthy foods supplemented with natural detoxifiers like fiber, leafy greens, herbs and spices like turmeric.

Myth 4: Foods labeled "natural" are healthier.

I learned this the hard way. For a long time, I thought the word "natural" meant no artificial chemicals. Then, I started reading the small print on the back of packages and bottles.

Oh boy. Was that an eye-opener.

Many foods with "natural," "wholesome," or "healthy" splashed across the front were loaded with bad fats, added sweeteners, genetically modified foods, and highly processed ingredients made in laboratories.

Manufacturers get away with false labeling because the regulations are weak. There are organizations and people lobbying the government to change these laws, but until that happens, let's take responsibility for our health and inform ourselves.

Read the ingredient list on the back before putting it in your mouth.

Myth 5: Diet foods keep us slim.

Foods labeled "low in fat" or "light" often contain harmful ingredients like added sweeteners or excessive salt to enhance taste. We should be especially careful of foods labeled "diet," as they're the most highly processed foods.

Studies have shown a correlation between the consumption of diet drinks and becoming overweight. Ironically, these so-called diet foods do the exact opposite of what they promise.

So let's not get fooled by these gimmicks. Let's stay informed and choose our products intelligently.

Myth 6: Eating healthy is expensive.

After switching from a rich meat-heavy diet to a plant-based diet, my grocery bills came down by fifty percent. Legumes, vegetables, fruit, and other whole foods cost a fraction of the price of processed foods or meat and dairy products.

You don't need to shop at über-pricey specialized grocery stores to get good food. Visit local farmers' markets, or better yet go to the farms directly if they're not too far away. It might even make for a pleasant Sunday drive for the family.

Browse smaller Chinese, Indian, and other "ethnic" stores in your neighborhood where prices are lower but the produce is the same. A trip to these stores will introduce you to new vegetables and exotic fruits.

If you're not the adventurous type, traditional chain stores are catching up to the growing health-food trend and are now offering healthy alternatives and produce in separate aisles. Make sure, though, to stay away from the center aisles that contain all the processed junk—which I call (silently to myself) the cancer corridors.

If you stick to a fully plant-based, whole foods, unrefined, *real* food diet, you'll get all the nutrients you need at a much lower cost.

HOW TO IMPROVE YOUR NUTRITION HEALTH

Since we're colored by our own biases and because many of us have a high emotional connection with the food we're used to, it can be hard to change. The least you can do is to find out where the information about your food is coming from, know how your food gets to your table, read the ingredient labels, and always be learning.

But eating well doesn't have to be painful. It's not rocket science either. The world-renowned nutritionist Michael Pollan said it best: "Eat food. Not too much. Mostly plants."

If we stick to this philosophy—it's a way of life, not a fad diet or trend—we'll arrive at our ideal personal body weight plus get the essential nutrients to stay healthy. The solution is simple. The mental shift we have to make is the hard part.

If we keep thinking it's impossible, we'll never improve. Such words will hold us back. They're excuses we make to stay as is. If you're serious about making a difference in your life, believe in yourself and tell yourself you can transform.

We can't make large-scale changes overnight, so give yourself time to adjust. Start with baby steps and make one small change every month.

THE STATE OF MY NUTRITION HEALTH TODAY

First, four key stock-taking questions.

---

1. How are you doing in this pillar of your life right now?

- ○ Great! I'm Super Woman at this.
- ○ Okay. I know things can be better but it's not too bad.
- ○ Not too well. I wish things were different.
- ○ Meh. I'm not at all interested in this area.

---

2. Why is this area of your life important to you right now?

---

3. Who around you will get inspired when you start taking care of this part of your life?

---

4. What is your one main goal for enhancing your nutrition health this year?

We'll talk about specific tips and actions you can take on the next page, but for now, set an overarching goal for this area of your life for this year.

"Ironically, the side effects of eating healthy can be not having to take (medical) drugs."
Dr. Michael Greger

MY NUTRITION HEALTH

TEN TIPS

1. EAT REAL FOOD

We need to eat real food again—food that looks like food, smells like food, and tastes like food.

Highly processed meat, dairy products, energy and soda drinks, or other food-like substances that come in tins, cans, cups, packets, packages, squeeze tubes and fast-food joints are mostly synthetic and formulated in a factory somewhere.

The easiest way to cut these foods out is to look up their ingredients. Most of the time, their labels have long, unpronounceable names. When you find the simulated sweeteners, artificial flavors, hormones, antibiotics, steroids, drugs, pesticides, coloring, saturated fats, trans fats, and other chemicalized concoctions, your stomach will turn.

This was what motivated me to move away from junk food.

Here's a tip to keep you healthy and safe. If you don't recognize the ingredients, maybe you shouldn't put it in your mouth.

There are no ingredient lists on fruits, vegetables, raw nuts, or grain bags for good reason. These are whole, fresh foods that humans have been eating for millennia, and they're what we're meant to eat. Once you switch to a whole foods, plant-based diet, you'll be astounded to realize you've forgotten what real food tastes like: fresh, sweet, succulent and flavorful.

2. GET MORE FRUITS AND VEGETABLES

Like our kindergarten teacher used to tell us, fruits and veggies are our best friends.

Plants are the richest sources of vitamins, minerals, and fiber—all of which are deficient in our modern diets. Plants contain hundreds of thousands of phytochemicals, many of which come with disease-fighting properties that a laboratory can't duplicate or put into a pill.

There are many supplements out there today touting the goodness of superfoods like blueberries and turmeric. None of them come cheap. Why not save your dollars and buy a small jar of real turmeric powder and add a teaspoon next time you cook a curry or make a stir-fry? Why not grab a handful of juicy blueberries instead of a blueberry pill?

Yes, it will take a few more minutes to stuff the berries in your mouth, chew them and swallow them versus taking a pill, but are we in that much of a rush we can't appreciate a simple fruit, one with all its natural ingredients intact?

We clear arable land to build factories and create synthetic stuff disguised as food, when we could have used that same piece of land to grow natural produce that is healthier for us and tastes better. Why do we live such artificial lives?

Let's eat as many real fruits and vegetables as we can, whenever we can. This will give us the necessary nutrition to stay healthy in the long term.

3. COOK AT HOME

I now prepare my meals the old-fashioned way, just like my Sri Lankan grandmother did.

This means I cook at home more often than not. I experiment with vegetables, nut and coconut milks, and use a variety of spices to add flavor instead of piling on the sugar and salt. By cooking at home, I know exactly what goes into my food. Plus, I reduce my grocery bills.

Every week, I scour the Internet for international recipes which makes me feel like I journey around the world with my meals. Cooking is not a chore anymore and I look forward to making meal plans on Sunday afternoons.

If you're still not convinced, cooking can be therapeutic, especially after a stressful day. It's also a great way to involve your family and have fun together. If you're not keen on cooking, think of it as a creative outlet where you get to play with ideas, try new things and de-stress while you're at it. I started cooking at the age of nine, so it's really child's play. Anyone can cook!

4. SEEK HEALTHIER PROTEINS

The World Health Organization recently classified red meat and processed meats as carcinogens. This came as a shock to many people but the good news is we have alternatives. Much healthier alternatives.

Whole grains, legumes, and vegetables are ample sources of good protein, plus they come without the health risks of the animal products.

If anyone tells you that protein only comes from meats, remember, the big beefy bull in the farmer's field gets all his essential nutrients, including protein, from a whole-food, plant-based diet. We too can get high-quality protein from the plants around us.

One myth that's been circulating for years is we don't have enough protein in our diets. But if you ask any physician in any modern city, they'll tell you we all get more than our share of proteins. Yes, *more*. They'll be hard pressed to remember when they had a patient come with a protein deficiency.

In fact, it's the opposite that's true. Many people who get ill miss important vitamins and minerals that come from vegetables and fruits. It's these nutrients that are severely lacking in our modern-day diets.

Beans, nuts, lentils, buckwheat, and soy are healthier protein substitutes which don't come with stomach-churning toxins, hormones, antibiotics, pus, blood, feces, and other contaminants hidden in meat products. Don't get fooled by the beautiful packaging in fancy grocery stores. Inform yourself of where your protein comes from and choose wisely.

5. PICK UP WHOLE FOODS

It always amazes me how we happily dole out our hard-earned money to buy food stripped of its nutrients. It's because we're addicted to the artificial flavors, sugars, and salt added to these products, but still, it's astonishing how we eagerly pay more to get *less*. Yes, you heard that right. We pay more money to buy lower-quality foods.

Whole foods are as close to their natural state as possible, and therefore dense in nutrients. These unprocessed foods are a far better option and more affordable than the highly refined and manufactured goods in stores.

Whole foods include fruits, vegetables, legumes, nuts, and bread, pasta and cereals made with whole grains. Eating a whole apple with its skin on is much better than apple juice, especially if it's supplemented with sugar and other unhealthy additives. The advantage of eating whole foods, like that apple, is they contain more fiber. Your body will be satisfied with less and you'll eat smaller portions. You'll also be regular and feel better every day.

Whenever you can, put whole foods in your shopping cart.

6. REDUCE YOUR PORTIONS

Our food portions are growing bigger and bigger. This used to be a North American trend, but we see this around the world now. People overstuff themselves with low-nutrient meals and then wonder how they become overweight. It's easy to connect the dots, but sadly, many would rather not.

When I was a child, my grandmother used to repeat a simple buddhist mantra that said stop eating when you're three-quarters full. This wasn't easy to do at first. But, here are two tricks I used to adopt this habit.

I use midsize dishes for lunches and suppers in place of regular dinner plates. I bought a set of beautifully designed smaller plates, which makes me feel like I'm dining at a fancy restaurant every day. These plates force me to serve less and not feel like I'm depriving myself.

The second trick stops me from piling on more servings, which I used to do before. Once I'm done with my meal, I tell myself that if I still feel hungry after clearing the table, I'll eat more. But every single time, I feel full by the time I get up and put the dishes away. I used to overeat because I didn't give my stomach the time to assess how full it was and relay that message to my brain.

These two simple tricks helped me cut down on portions without feeling like I was giving up on anything. Try them and see how it goes.

7. BUY ORGANIC SELECTIVELY

Organic foods are sweeter and tastier because they conserve their natural flavors better. Even more important, organic produce comes without toxic pesticides laced all over it.

Eating organic doesn't have to cost you heaven and earth. Here's one tip to keep your grocery bills in check.

Every year, I go to the Environmental Working Group's website and look up their annual Dirty Dozen list. They create this list after testing hundreds of produce for toxins and pesticides and from looking at trends in food production and agri-business. I note the worst offenders, those tested high for toxicity, and buy them in the more expensive organic aisle. I buy the remaining fruits and vegetables safely in the regular aisles and avoid spending a fortune on my grocery bills.

Here's a link to the website of the Environmental Working Group. www.ewg.org

You can find the Dirty Dozen list right here: (www.ewg.org/foodnews/dirty_dozen_list.php#.Wlwad6inFhE)

8. ELIMINATE THE BAD STUFF

The most unhealthy culprits in our foods are sugar, salt, and bad fats.

Sugar has almost no nutritional value and is harmful to our liver. It's known to increase the risk of obesity, heart disease, diabetes, and cancer. Studies also show that sugar may be linked to cognitive degenerative diseases like Alzheimer's and dementia. This is scary if you think of how much of it we put in our bodies every day.

Unlike sugar, salt is necessary for our bodies to function. Problems arise when we over-consume it in our modern diets. Both salt and sugar are used heavily to mask the real taste of processed junk foods, and these additives are the main reason we crave unhealthy bad foods.

Not all fats are bad. Trans fats and saturated fats that come from poultry skin, red meat, dairy products, margarine, and commercially processed foods can be harmful to us. In contrast, monosaturated fats from plant-based foods like walnuts, almonds, chia seeds, flax seeds, avocado, coconut, and olives are good for our health, especially our brain health.

So here's the verdict: choose your fats carefully, reduce your salt intake, and avoid sugar as much as possible.

Once you retrain your taste buds by eating real food for a few days, you'll automatically stop craving the bad stuff.

9. DRINK MORE WATER

We all know we must cut out sugary drinks and reduce our consumption of alcohol, but we shouldn't stop there.

Sixty percent of the human body is composed of water. Water plays a crucial role in preserving our bodily functions and nurtures the health of our organs, cells, and tissue. Our digestion, blood circulation, waste removal, body temperature, and skin health all require good old-fashioned water. So it's imperative we keep ourselves hydrated.

I've noticed that whenever I drink more than two liters of water a day, my skin feels softer and my face looks brighter and younger, to the point people comment on it. This is a personal anecdote and not supported by any scientific studies. But why not replace sugary colas and highly chemicalized energy drinks with simple water for two weeks and see what it does to your skin? I think you'll like what you see.

Drink water when you're thirsty and drink lots of it. Make sure to drink one full glass of cool water first thing after you wake up to start your day refreshed.

10. UPGRADE YOUR MINDSET

Here's one of the greatest modern-day dilemmas: everybody wants to lose weight, but nobody wants to eat healthily.

Many friends of mine run after a new fad diet every year. Some have even tried liposuction and other intrusive surgeries to get thin fast with disastrous outcomes. The results never last and at times backfire by making them sicker.

I know this is not a popular thing to say, and some of you probably want to fling this book out the window by now. In my defense, I did put a warning cautioning anyone who doesn't want look truth in the face.

So, what's the truth here? When we eat a nutritious diet of plant-based whole foods, we naturally realize our optimum body size. Yes! In contrast, fad diets harm us more than help us and may even cause weight gain in the long run. There, I've said it. You can throw this book out now.

Still here?

Okay, the problem many of us face is we imagine our "ideal" weight to be that of the anorexic runway model on the catwalk in Milan, when in fact that image is unrealistic and unhealthy. If you spotted the image in a glossy magazine it has certainly been photoshopped to death. Most of these fashion models live extremely unhealthy lifestyles anyway—not ones we'd want to emulate if we want long and happy lives free from stress and disease.

We must remember that we, women, come in different shapes, sizes, ages, and races. We can't all look the same and we need to stop believing what the media and magazines push on us. We must learn to ignore these external critics and eat balanced nutrient-dense meals.

Healthy is the new skinny.

Bonus Tip

11. DO IT FOR MOTHER EARTH

Do you care for the planet? Would you like your children and your grandchildren to thrive in healthy environments and enjoy the natural beauty around them?

If you do, before you blame the industrialists, the car manufacturers, the governments and the lobbyists for the environmental degradation happening around us, look at your plate first.

Did you know the meat, dairy, and fishing industries are the biggest offenders of the environmental problems we're facing today? Livestock production is responsible for more clear-cutting of forests, greenhouse gas emissions, and pollution of our air and freshwater lakes and rivers than most other sectors. The numbers are horrendous, and that's without counting the harm we're doing to our oceans.

Companies don't pollute the environment for fun. They exist to meet consumer demand and make profits from that. They'll continue to give what we ask for and what we're willing to pay for. Corporations must absolutely take on their part of social responsibility, but we can't point a finger at them with one hand while stuffing their products into our mouths with the other.

No need to take it from me. I'd recommend you do your own research and inform yourself. Find out where your food comes from. Ask how your daily diet affects the quality of the air you breathe, the water you drink and the land you stand on. Think about the legacy you're leaving your next generations because of the food you put into your mouth three times a day.

If you honestly want to make a difference in the world, start with your plate.

THE HABIT MAKER

Let's Make These Stick

Pick one idea from the tips list and try it out for one month. Do this for thirty days and see how you do. Then, if you can, try a new one next month.

So, what is *one* action you'll take to incorporate nutrition health into your life this month?

Go back to the annual goal you set at the start of this section and make sure the activity you choose links to your goals.

Set January Activity:
Track the Activity: Check back at the end of the month to see how well you did
○ Great! I was Super Woman at this. ○ Good. I managed this most of the time. ○ Okay, I guess. I know I can get better. ○ Not so well. So, maybe I need to try this again. Who said you have to get it right the first time.
How can I improve next month?

Your Rebel Life

Set February Activity:

Track the Activity: Check back at the end of the month to see how well you did

- ○ Great! I was Super Woman at this.
- ○ Good. I managed this most of the time.
- ○ Okay, I guess. I know I can get better.
- ○ Not so well. So, maybe I need to try this again. Who said you have to get it right the first time.

How can I improve next month?

Set March Activity:

Track the Activity: Check back at the end of the month to see how well you did

- ○ Great! I was Super Woman at this.
- ○ Good. I managed this most of the time.
- ○ Okay, I guess. I know I can get better.
- ○ Not so well. So, maybe I need to try this again. Who said you have to get it right the first time.

How can I improve next month?

Set April Activity:
Track the Activity: Check back at the end of the month to see how well you did

- ○ Great! I was Super Woman at this.
- ○ Good. I managed this most of the time.
- ○ Okay, I guess. I know I can get better.
- ○ Not so well. So, maybe I need to try this again. Who said you have to get it right the first time.

How can I improve next month?

Set May Activity:
Track the Activity: Check back at the end of the month to see how well you did

- ○ Great! I was Super Woman at this.
- ○ Good. I managed this most of the time.
- ○ Okay, I guess. I know I can get better.
- ○ Not so well. So, maybe I need to try this again. Who said you have to get it right the first time.

How can I improve next month?

Set June Activity:

Track the Activity: Check back at the end of the month to see how well you did

- ◯ Great! I was Super Woman at this.
- ◯ Good. I managed this most of the time.
- ◯ Okay, I guess. I know I can get better.
- ◯ Not so well. So, maybe I need to try this again. Who said you have to get it right the first time.

How can I improve next month?

Set July Activity:

Track the Activity: Check back at the end of the month to see how well you did

- ◯ Great! I was Super Woman at this.
- ◯ Good. I managed this most of the time.
- ◯ Okay, I guess. I know I can get better.
- ◯ Not so well. So, maybe I need to try this again. Who said you have to get it right the first time.

How can I improve next month?

Set August Activity:

Track the Activity: Check back at the end of the month to see how well you did

- ○ Great! I was Super Woman at this.
- ○ Good. I managed this most of the time.
- ○ Okay, I guess. I know I can get better.
- ○ Not so well. So, maybe I need to try this again. Who said you have to get it right the first time.

How can I improve next month?

Set September Activity:

Track the Activity: Check back at the end of the month to see how well you did

- ○ Great! I was Super Woman at this.
- ○ Good. I managed this most of the time.
- ○ Okay, I guess. I know I can get better.
- ○ Not so well. So, maybe I need to try this again. Who said you have to get it right the first time.

How can I improve next month?

Set October Activity:

Track the Activity: Check back at the end of the month to see how well you did

- ○ Great! I was Super Woman at this.
- ○ Good. I managed this most of the time.
- ○ Okay, I guess. I know I can get better.
- ○ Not so well. So, maybe I need to try this again. Who said you have to get it right the first time.

How can I improve next month?

Set November Activity:

Track the Activity: Check back at the end of the month to see how well you did

- ○ Great! I was Super Woman at this.
- ○ Good. I managed this most of the time.
- ○ Okay, I guess. I know I can get better.
- ○ Not so well. So, maybe I need to try this again. Who said you have to get it right the first time.

How can I improve next month?

Set December Activity:
Track the Activity: Check back at the end of the month to see how well you did
○ Great! I was Super Woman at this. ○ Good. I managed this most of the time. ○ Okay, I guess. I know I can get better. ○ Not so well. So, maybe I need to try this again. Who said you have to get it right the first time.
How can I improve next month?

SO, HOW DO YOU FEEL?

That's the end of this section. What do you think of the answers you gave here? If something wasn't captured in this section but you want to get it out of your system, this is the place to do so.

_____

_____

_____

_____

_____

_____

_____

_____

_____

Tikiri

Your Rebel Life

SECTION FIVE
LEARN WELL

Knowledge Health

"Find who you are in this world and what you need to feel good alone. I think that's the most important thing in life. Find a sense of self. With that, you can do anything else."

Angelina Jolie

"Learn from yesterday, live for today, hope for tomorrow. The important thing is not to stop questioning."

Albert Einstein

LEARN WELL

Our Knowledge Health

WHAT I'VE LEARNED ABOUT LEARNING WELL

Do you know the first thing that happens when a malevolent dictator takes over a country?

Time and time again, history has shown us that oppressive regimes target those who share knowledge. It's the journalists, the storytellers, the filmmakers, and the news publishers who get muzzled during hostile takeovers. Writers have it bad too. They tend to get carted off, imprisoned, or tortured, which means I'm in a career where I'd be in line to "disappear" if Canada ever got terrorized by an evil dictator…

Why is this so?

When you gain knowledge, especially from diverse sources, you become a critical thinker. You start asking questions. You start critiquing ideas and looking at concepts from different angles. You start wondering about the status quo and may even contemplate how to make things better. And you start sharing your ideas with those around you. You won't be able to help it.

Your mind's doing what a healthy, intelligent, and highly evolved human brain is designed to do. And this is a dangerous thing for any despot who wants to keep you or a society down.

WOMEN AROUND THE WORLD

That's ancient history, you might say. *How is this information relevant to me?*

Do you know in this twenty-first century, there are over 500 million women in the world who can't read or write? That's two-thirds of the global illiterate population. These are the poorest humans on Earth and the most vulnerable to violence and abuse. Do you wonder why women make up such an inordinate portion of this sad statistic?

Let me share another fact.

According to a recent UNESCO study, 130 million girls around the world who should be in school are not. Yes, you read that right. One hundred and thirty million girls—three and a half times the population of Canada or equivalent to the total population of Mexico at the time this book was written—are denied a basic primary education. How does such a travesty happen?

While we may wish it were not true, many cultures still value a girl much less than a boy.

These cultures have societal norms and even laws that take away a woman's right to education, speech, expression, and movement. Girls are seen as being good for three things: an unpaid housemaid, a baby-making vessel or an emotionless creature to be used for sexual pleasure.

Margaret Atwood's Handmaid's Tale is no dystopian fantasy. It's a documentary of what's happening around us right now. In the 21st century.

These families forbid their daughters to read books, watch television, browse the Internet, finish school, or socialize outside the family warning they'll get "corrupted." Interestingly, the male members are freely allowed, if not encouraged, all these "corrupting" freedoms and more.

Why do I bring this up? You may think this has nothing to do with you, let alone a chapter on the power of knowledge.

The point I'm trying to make is this. The most effective way to keep another human being down is to keep them ignorant.

It was no accident that young Malala from Pakistan was shot for wanting to go to school. The extent to which misogynistic cultures go to cripple school girls says a lot about the power of knowledge. Doesn't it?

OUR OPPORTUNITY

Those of us, especially us women, in modern and open societies are fortunate in more ways than we can imagine.

We've won the lottery of life to live in the free world. Yet, how many of us would rather sit on a couch and watch a reality show than learn something new? How many of us peruse social media mindlessly for countless hours (I've been guilty) rather than read a book, take a course, watch an educational video or try their hand at something new?

We take our freedoms for granted without realizing that half a world away, there are women who'd trade places with us in a heartbeat. Just to read a book.

Isn't it then our responsibility to make use of what we have?

When we gain knowledge, enhance our skills, gain new experiences, and become more aware of what's around us, we become role models for the rest of the world. Taking accountability for our learning is the least we can do, not just for ourselves but for our less fortunate sisters elsewhere.

Prioritizing our learning and cultivating a growth mindset are the most effective ways to stand in our own power.

Learning is the best way to avoid being pushed around or manipulated. When we become knowledgeable, it's more difficult for others to lie, cheat or deceive us. They may still try, but they'll have to work harder, knowing we're critical thinkers used to asking questions and not prone to taking BS.

DIVERSE SOURCES

Getting an education doesn't necessarily mean a university degree.

In fact, higher education institutions can at times hinder rather than help success. Our formal education system was built to create nineteenth-century factory workers. It wasn't designed to foster a thinking, inquiring, or learning population. This is changing, but progress is slow.

In the meantime, we can self-teach by reading books, modeling others, trying things out or starting projects on our own. The Internet has democratized knowledge, which means we have almost all the information in the world in the palm of our hands. There's no excuse not to explore and learn more.

We shouldn't completely rule out formal education. Basic primary, middle and high school are all highly important. After that, we have choices. We can go to a trade school and apprentice to become a plumber. Or, we can go to an engineering school and learn how to build buildings and bridges. Our post-secondary options are endless, and none is inherently better than the other.

All we have to do is find what feeds our passions and follow that.

GROWTH MINDSET

No matter which path we choose, the one trait that will help us succeed is having an enduring growth mindset.

Cultivate a continual thirst for knowledge. Stay curious and don't be afraid of becoming a beginner again. That's the best way to learn something new. It's also a great way to learn how to learn.

The capacity of the human mind is infinite. Our intelligence isn't fixed.

We can improve in all areas of our lives regardless of our birthplace, family, background, environment or experiences. We can learn whether we're nine years old or ninety-nine.

BENEFITS OF LEARNING

So, what are the benefits of being a lifelong learner? Let's count the ways.

Having a learning mindset:

- Sharpens our brains and expands our knowledge.
- Increases our competency and our confidence.
- Makes us independent and gives us more authority.
- Makes us more well-rounded and open-minded.
- Increases our productivity and the quality of our work.
- Reduces the probability of us making mistakes.
- Increases our chances for success in our careers and lives.
- Makes us better leaders.
- Reduces the chances of others taking advantage of us or even trying to harm us.
- Reduces boredom, stagnation, and depression.
- Slows the aging of our brains.
- Reduces the risk of cognitive degenerative diseases, like dementia and Alzheimer's.
- Gives us fulfilled and rewarding lives.

So why wouldn't we want to always be learning?

OUR CULTURE

Over the past few decades, the media has bombarded us with images of the stereotypical empty-headed but "cute" girl as the one who can attract a man.

I didn't realize how ingrained this thinking was until George Clooney married international human rights lawyer Amal Alamuddin. Morning radio shows and entertainment TV shows cackled with talk of how the sexiest man alive had settled for a "smart" woman. "See that, boys," quipped one show host, "Go for the smart chicks."

In recent years, we're seeing a reversal in this thinking, at least in North America. The pendulum is swinging to the other extreme, and it's men who are now being portrayed as the clueless ones on television.

Neither perspective is healthy or true. Playing dumb, whether you're a woman or a man, is not attractive. Plus, it's enormously harmful to our self-esteem and self-confidence.

So stay curious. Don't be afraid to ask questions, learn new things and show off your knowledge.

Smart is the new sexy.

THE STATE OF MY KNOWLEDGE HEALTH TODAY

First, four key stock-taking questions.

1. How are you doing in this pillar of your life right now?

- ○ Great! I'm Super Woman at this.
- ○ Okay. I know things can be better but it's not too bad.
- ○ Not too well. I wish things were different.
- ○ Meh. I'm not at all interested in this area.

2. Why is this area of your life important to you right now?

3. Who around you will get inspired when you start taking care of this part of your life?

4. What is your one main goal for enhancing your knowledge health this year?

We'll talk about specific tips and actions you can take on the next page, but for now, set an overarching goal for this area of your life for this year.

Your Rebel Life

"The more that you read, the more things you will know. The more that you learn, the more places you'll go."
Dr. Seuss

MY KNOWLEDGE HEALTH

TEN TIPS

1. FOLLOW YOUR PASSIONS

If you're passionate about a topic, learning about it won't feel like a chore. So, how do we discover our passions then?

One way is to recall what you were keen on and dreamed about when you were nine years old. You may have given up on that interest as you grew older and adult responsibilities took over. But sometimes what we enjoyed in our childhood could be what brings the most joy into our lives today. It's never too late to revive these passions of ours.

Your Rebel Dreams, the first Rebel Diva workbook, has a series of tests you can take to identify your passions. Here are seven quick suggestions from those exercises:

- Think about what you gravitate to when you have free time.
- Ask yourself what you'd do even if you never got paid a dime.
- Think about the times when you felt most authentic and true to yourself.
- Think about what you daydream and see if you can make those dreams a reality.

- Make an inventory of your skills and knowledge and look for areas where your interests are highest.
- Look for activities that put you in the flow where the world recedes around you and you happily focus on this one thing.
- Experiment with different topics to discover what you enjoy most. Go wide to start. You can go deep once you've found your true passions.

Reread that first workbook and go through the exercises if you haven't found your passions yet. Answer the questions truthfully and you may uncover your purpose in life!

2. USE DIVERSE SOURCES

Whenever I come across an interesting subject, I get hungry for knowledge. I scour for books, articles, blogs, podcasts, videos, and experts in that field. Then I read, listen, and watch them all. This way, I get to understand the nuances, the conflicts, and the controversies of the topic. When I do this, I find myself years ahead of someone who has been doing the same old thing in that field for years.

We should never take what others say for granted and not be afraid to learn from as many diverse perspectives as possible.

Make sure you're not studying only one methodology, one process, or one idea about anything. Seek information from as many different areas as possible. Explore the topic and make up your own mind about what works or doesn't.

As you learn, ask yourself if things can be done differently, if disparate ideas can come together to create a whole new concept, or if an old idea can be implemented in a new field to create something brand new. This is how innovation happens. You're in the best position to innovate when you're still learning, as your mind is open and curious.

At the end of this book, I share a list of fifty thought-leaders and fifty books you can tap into so you can make up your own mind about the topics provided here. Don't take anything anyone says as gospel—even from me!

3. BE MINDFUL

We may not realize it, but we're learning all the time. We glean information subconsciously when we're reading a novel, watching a movie, listening to a podcast, or even spotting a billboard ad while we're driving. All these instill information in our brains without us even realizing it.

The question you need to ask is; is this the kind of knowledge you want to gain?

Be discerning of what you're absorbing, or you could unintentionally seed ideas, thoughts, and attitudes that could have a negative impact on your mental and physical health, your relationships or even future goals.

This means being aware of your surroundings, the people you spend time with, and the information you consume. Learn to spot advertisements geared to sell, rhetoric shared to provoke emotions and superficial trends of the day, and see them for what they are. Seek evidenced-based information that looks at all sides of a topic.

This is one good reason to limit the time we watch or read the news. The news media thrives on crises, and if we dwell on these, we can easily (and wrongly) conclude the world is a depressing place.

Become clear on what you want to learn, from where you want to learn it, and how you'll use what you learn in a positive and progressive way. Stay mindful of what information your brain is absorbing.

4. KNOW YOUR LEARNING STYLE

Everybody learns differently.

Some people need to see an image for a concept to sink into their minds. Others learn while listening to someone speak about a topic. Then, there are those who must touch, feel, and experience something to learn it.

Most of us use a combination of visual, auditory, and tactical ways of learning. It's important to know how you learn best and apply the most effective methods to pick up new skills.

In the same way, consider the environments in which you learn best. Some of us do well on our own and prefer not to be disturbed. Others learn better when they're surrounded by people who also learn by interacting with each other.

Ask yourself; what are your learning patterns and preferences? Identify these to maximize your absorption and retention rates.

5. SET GOALS AND MAKE A PLAN

In January, I set one annual goal for each of the ten pillars of my life—from mental, physical and spiritual health, to career, relationships, finances and more. Parallel to this, I come up with one learning idea related to each of these goals.

Think about what you plan to accomplish this year. Then ask yourself what you must do to meet your goals. Look at your existing skills and knowledge and consider the training you'll need. Then, seek it out whether it's via formal courses (example: a personal finance online program) or self-teaching exercises (example: a book or podcast on how to become more mindful).

As with any plan, your learning plan needs timelines, milestones, and the specific results you want to achieve. Otherwise, it becomes a mere wish list that gets quickly waylaid to collect dust.

There's a wise saying that "what gets measured, gets done."

Tracking your learning plan regularly will help you get results faster. Your Rebel Plans, the second book in the Rebel Diva series, has a tracking table to check up on your plans. You can use that tool, a variation of it or any other mechanism to check your progress.

Whatever tool you use, tracking your plan systematically is a powerful motivator to achieving your learning goals. When you achieve your learning goals, you'll, in turn, advance your life goals.

6. PRIORITIZE LEARNING

Marketing and business guru Seth Godin found out that most online courses have a ninety-seven percent drop-off rate. Most people stop at the second module when they realize they have to put in work or because they got distracted by a shiny object. This is a very expensive way to not learn something.

Scheduling your learning activities on an online or paper calendar is a great way to stay disciplined. When you slot an activity on your daily calendar, it's a reminder of what you've decided to do.

It's easy to sacrifice learning to other life priorities. Setting a specific time for learning on a daily or weekly basis will make sure it stays on your radar and doesn't get dropped off.

Find at least fifteen minutes every day or an hour on a Sunday afternoon to dedicate to your learning activities. Put alerts or alarms on your phone or laptop to remind you when to start so you won't have any excuse.

Find a quiet spot and make sure others know not to interrupt you. Remove all distractions and concentrate on the learning task. If social media constantly pulls you away, use an Internet blocker like www.freedom.to that will turn off your connection and force you to focus. Use brain-stimulating music to help you stay in your zone. YouTube has many playlists made just for this.

One helpful practice is to do a five-minute meditation before starting a learning activity. This will remove the clutter in your head and allow you to get into the right frame of mind so you can absorb what you're learning.

Prioritize learning.

7. BROWSE WISELY

We can use our online devices to watch funny dash cam videos and kittens playing with laser dots. Or, we can use them to expand our minds and enhance our knowledge. It's a choice.

If you think about it, the Internet and all its related technologies are the greatest inventions of humankind. If anyone time-traveled from the nineteenth century, they'd be stupefied and think it's all magic. And magic it is.

These amazing innovations have given us an ever-expanding global channel to connect with people across the world in a matter of seconds. We can learn just about anything on any subject on Earth faster than ever before. Yet, a majority of us waste it by watching puppy videos or arguing with strangers online.

It's up to us to choose who we connect with, how we use these technologies, and for what purpose. Let's use it sensibly.

8. TAKE ACTION

Apply what you learn.

Regular and repeated practice is crucial to embedding knowledge in our brains. By taking action, even those of us who learn solely through visual or auditory means can ingrain new information more deeply in our conscience.

We may read an article, listen to a podcast or watch a video, but after that, we must roll up our sleeves and *do it*. We need to make the recipe, write the essay, do the lab experiment, carve the piece of wood, or fix the kitchen tap, so we can learn it faster and remember it in the long-term.

Taking action is one step to enhance our learning. The second is to not be afraid to make mistakes.

Back in the nineteenth century, Thomas Edison was asked by a snarky colleague about his many failed attempts at inventing the light bulb. Here's how Edison replied: "I didn't have one thousand failures. I had to try it a thousand ways before getting it right." Take that, snarky colleague!

Our first attempts at anything will be the hardest. That's when we must knuckle down and test, fail and test again. As cliché as this sounds, a mistake is never a true failure when you learn something that will get you closer to your goal. If we can adopt Edison's perspective, we just might banish the word failure from our vocabulary.

The trick is to never strive for perfection as that is a killer of success. You're better off starting something than sitting around waiting for the "perfect" solution. Perfection is never attainable, and neither should it be. Done is always better than perfect.

Remember, everyone has to begin somewhere, so stop waiting for the right time or the right moment or right muse, and start. *Now*.

9. TEACH OTHERS

Teaching is a wonderful way to learn.

When we educate others on a topic we're familiar with, we get back into the beginner's mindset. This allows us to see things we may not have observed before and go in-depth into areas we may not have explored earlier.

Whenever I'm asked to teach, I re-examine the basic building blocks of the topic and ask fundamental questions I'd not have asked otherwise. I also find myself thinking about the subject more deeply and looking for the right words to explain it better—all of which strengthens my own knowledge in the area.

Teaching others a subject you know well can make it exciting for you again. You can come up with fun ways to impart your knowledge and enjoy seeing others learn and grow. Try it.

10. TRUST YOUR BRAIN

One of our culture's biggest misconceptions is that we stop learning somewhere in middle age.

Given our extended lifespans these days, age fifty-five is merely the halfway point of our lives. Things are just getting interesting!

One woman I know bucked current trends and entered medical school in her fifties, instead of retiring. Her childhood dream had been to become a physician and she didn't want to die with that regret. Age, to her, wasn't a limitation. In fact, it didn't seem to bother her at all.

Her friends cautioned her about being singled out or getting ridiculed for sitting in a class with twenty-year-olds, but she didn't care one bit. She's now happily doing the thing many said she couldn't or shouldn't do. She's one of many women who've changed careers and achieved new levels of success later on in their lives.

What keeps us from following in the footsteps of this brave woman? Is it a mindset that our brains are fixed? Is it a false assumption that after a certain age it's too late to learn anything new?

The truth is our brains are elastic and flexible, capable of expanding every day regardless of age, how well we did at school, what others say or even a head injury we may grapple with.

You've probably heard the neuroscience theory of plasticity. This states that our brains are malleable and can grow and adjust continually. So, it's never too late. We must embrace a growth mindset and leap from one amazing adventure to the next, continuing to learn and have fun until the day we let out our last breath.

THE HABIT MAKER

Let's Make These Stick

Pick one idea from the tips list and try it out for one month. Do this for thirty days and see how you do. Then, if you can, try a new one next month.

So, what is *one* action you'll take to incorporate knowledge growth into your life this month?

Go back to the annual goal you set at the start of this section and make sure the activity you choose links to your goals.

Set January Activity:
Track the Activity: Check back at the end of the month to see how well you did
○ Great! I was Super Woman at this.
○ Good. I managed this most of the time.
○ Okay, I guess. I know I can get better.
○ Not so well. So, maybe I need to try this again. Who said you have to get it right the first time.
How can I improve next month?

Set February Activity:

Track the Activity: Check back at the end of the month to see how well you did

- ○ Great! I was Super Woman at this.
- ○ Good. I managed this most of the time.
- ○ Okay, I guess. I know I can get better.
- ○ Not so well. So, maybe I need to try this again. Who said you have to get it right the first time.

How can I improve next month?

Set March Activity:

Track the Activity: Check back at the end of the month to see how well you did

- ○ Great! I was Super Woman at this.
- ○ Good. I managed this most of the time.
- ○ Okay, I guess. I know I can get better.
- ○ Not so well. So, maybe I need to try this again. Who said you have to get it right the first time.

How can I improve next month?

Set April Activity:

Track the Activity: Check back at the end of the month to see how well you did

- ○ Great! I was Super Woman at this.
- ○ Good. I managed this most of the time.
- ○ Okay, I guess. I know I can get better.
- ○ Not so well. So, maybe I need to try this again. Who said you have to get it right the first time.

How can I improve next month?

Set May Activity:

Track the Activity: Check back at the end of the month to see how well you did

- ○ Great! I was Super Woman at this.
- ○ Good. I managed this most of the time.
- ○ Okay, I guess. I know I can get better.
- ○ Not so well. So, maybe I need to try this again. Who said you have to get it right the first time.

How can I improve next month?

Set June Activity:

Track the Activity: Check back at the end of the month to see how well you did

- ○ Great! I was Super Woman at this.
- ○ Good. I managed this most of the time.
- ○ Okay, I guess. I know I can get better.
- ○ Not so well. So, maybe I need to try this again. Who said you have to get it right the first time.

How can I improve next month?

Set July Activity:

Track the Activity: Check back at the end of the month to see how well you did

- ○ Great! I was Super Woman at this.
- ○ Good. I managed this most of the time.
- ○ Okay, I guess. I know I can get better.
- ○ Not so well. So, maybe I need to try this again. Who said you have to get it right the first time.

How can I improve next month?

Set August Activity:
Track the Activity: Check back at the end of the month to see how well you did
○ Great! I was Super Woman at this. ○ Good. I managed this most of the time. ○ Okay, I guess. I know I can get better. ○ Not so well. So, maybe I need to try this again. Who said you have to get it right the first time.
How can I improve next month?

Set September Activity:
Track the Activity: Check back at the end of the month to see how well you did
○ Great! I was Super Woman at this. ○ Good. I managed this most of the time. ○ Okay, I guess. I know I can get better. ○ Not so well. So, maybe I need to try this again. Who said you have to get it right the first time.
How can I improve next month?

Set October Activity:

Track the Activity: Check back at the end of the month to see how well you did

- ○ Great! I was Super Woman at this.
- ○ Good. I managed this most of the time.
- ○ Okay, I guess. I know I can get better.
- ○ Not so well. So, maybe I need to try this again. Who said you have to get it right the first time.

How can I improve next month?

Set November Activity:

Track the Activity: Check back at the end of the month to see how well you did

- ○ Great! I was Super Woman at this.
- ○ Good. I managed this most of the time.
- ○ Okay, I guess. I know I can get better.
- ○ Not so well. So, maybe I need to try this again. Who said you have to get it right the first time.

How can I improve next month?

Set December Activity:
Track the Activity: Check back at the end of the month to see how well you did
○ Great! I was Super Woman at this. ○ Good. I managed this most of the time. ○ Okay, I guess. I know I can get better. ○ Not so well. So, maybe I need to try this again. Who said you have to get it right the first time.
How can I improve next month?

SO, HOW DO YOU FEEL?

That's the end of this section. What do you think of the answers you gave here? If something wasn't captured in this section but you want to get it out of your system, this is the place to do so.

_____

_____

_____

_____

_____

_____

_____

_____

_____

_____

Tikiri

Your Rebel Life

SECTION SIX

WORK WELL

Career Health

"You can have unbelievable intellirgence, you can have connections, you can have opportunities fall out of the sky. But in the end, hard work is the true, enduring characteristic of successful people."

Marsha Evans

"You can only become truly accomplished at something you love. Don't make money your goal. Instead, pursue the things you love doing, and then do them so well that people can't take their eyes off you."
Maya Angelou

WORK WELL

Our Career Health

This section provides a brief summary of the first two Rebel Diva books. For details and worksheet guides, look at *Your Rebel Dreams* and *Your Rebel Plans*. Skip this section if you've already gone through these first books.

WHAT I'VE LEARNED ABOUT WORKING WELL

Recent studies show that eighty percent of North Americans are unhappy in their jobs. A third absolutely detest their work.

Shocking statistics. But it's so commonplace to hate your job or your boss now we think the guy or girl who loves their work is the weird one.

This workplace unhappiness is becoming a global phenomena as more people enter the race to get that fancy car, that big house, and that perfect lifestyle they presume the Joneses next door to have.

When the world has more women and men seeking higher education, striving for well-paying jobs, and enhancing their standard of living, the entire human race moves forward. This is a good thing. This is an absolutely fantastic thing.

But it seems we may have taken a wrong turn somewhere because we're increasingly sacrificing our health, happiness, and relationships in this never-ending quest for status and wealth.

We invest a significant amount of time, energy and sweat in work that doesn't give us meaning. We spend far more time with strangers than with our families, in environments we don't like, doing work we don't enjoy. Some of us may even take on two or three jobs to pay the bills.

IS WORK AN ESSENTIAL EVIL?

One of the biggest myths of this brave new world is that working is an essential evil. Many believe work, by its very nature, is drudgery.

"You don't have to like what you do, but it pays the mortgage" is a comment I hear often. "You gotta do what you gotta do" is another remark mostly touted by men and a growing number of women. If you think this way, you've already set yourself up to fail.

I believe work can be fulfilling and fun if we choose right.

CHOOSE RIGHT

Can a job truly be enjoyable and still pay the rent?

If you believe you can't make a living doing what you love, think about the many multi-million-dollar athletes, magicians, fine artists, opera singers, songwriters, novelists, fashion designers, and these days, even yoga instructors and YouTube video creators who are doing extremely well.

Their success results from embracing their passions, creating a vision, setting goals, refining their craft, practicing their skill, and working damn hard—harder than anyone else in their industry. They never gave up in their quest for success.

But many people don't want to exert this effort. They'd rather give up, sometimes before even starting. Then, they go around telling everybody that dreaming is for wimps. Their only option is to work at jobs they detest, ironically helping to fulfill other people's dreams.

The eighty percent who say they're unhappy in their work have merely chosen the wrong path.

They bowed to demands from their parents, teachers, or a society that said they had a narrow road to take, one paved by the many who'd gone before them. Someone, somewhere, told them that veering off this predetermined route would lead to failure or loss of status.

So they trailed after the herd into soul-crushing jobs and found themselves shackled for life. They now have no choice but to continue doing work they don't enjoy so they can pay for the things they bought to fill the hole in their souls.

I was one of these herd followers, so I know exactly how this feels.

MAKE IT MEANINGFUL

What if there is a way to find meaningful work we love doing? What if we can do work that won't feel like "work"?

Imagine if we engaged in activities aligned with our personal purpose and passions. Imagine if our work made a positive difference in our lives and the lives of others. How happy would we be? Now imagine a world where everybody can discover their North Star and live with this freedom.

I don't think this is an impossible dream.

It's when we find work we love that we become good at it. It motivates us to work harder, which, in turn, allows us to reap emotional benefits and financial rewards. This becomes a virtuous cycle that feeds our minds, bodies, and souls.

But a warning. If we want to go down this unpaved path where few dare to tread, we must seek courage. We must look deep within ourselves and ask what's most important to us. We must move away from the naysayers. We must strategize and plan. And we must persevere through our failures. And failures will happen.

This won't be a painless undertaking, but it's not unattainable. If it were easy, everybody would be doing it.

So, how can we start living a life of passionate work?

The first Rebel Diva workbook, *Your Rebel Dreams,* tackles this topic head-on. In it, you'll find a series of exercises designed to uncover your purpose and passions in life. It will also show you how to create a vision based on the work you enjoy doing. The second Rebel Diva workbook, *Your Rebel Plans,* gives the necessary planning tools to make your passions come alive.

The next part of this section shares a summary from both these books.

THE STATE OF MY CAREER HEALTH TODAY

First, four key stock-taking questions.

1. How are you doing in this pillar of your life right now?

- ○ Great! I'm Super Woman at this.
- ○ Okay. I know things can be better but it's not too bad.
- ○ Not too well. I wish things were different.
- ○ Meh. I'm not at all interested in this area.

2. Why is this area of your life important to you right now?

3. Who around you will get inspired when you start taking care of this part of your life?

4. What is your one main goal for enhancing your career health this year?

We'll talk about specific tips and actions you can take on the next page, but for now, set an overarching goal for this area of your life for this year.

"Our job in this lifetime is not to shape ourselves into some ideal we imagine we ought to be, but to find out who we already are and become it."
Steven Pressfield

THE PASSION PYRAMID AND THE SWEET SPOT

The tips in this section are based on the Passion Pyramid and the Sweet Spot that were introduced in the first two workbooks of the Rebel Diva series.

What you'll see here is a synopsis of the ideas and concepts of those two first books. If you'd like to follow the lessons in their entirety and get access to all the exercises, you may want to pick up the first two Rebel Diva workbooks and dedicate a few quiet minutes to answering the questions there.

THE PASSION PYRAMID

So, what is the Passion Pyramid?

The Passion Pyramid shows how your values, your goals, your habits and lifestyle fit together. Ultimately, your vision in life is based on your personal values, your goals are derived from your vision, and your plans come out of your goals. Your vision, goals, and plans are all sustained by your daily habits, and if aligned well, will take you toward the life you dream about.

THE SWEET SPOT

Your sweet spot is where your passions meet your foundational needs. These needs include doing meaningful work you enjoy and are good at, working in environments where you thrive in, and being able to give value to the world around you.

If you can make your way into this special spot—the intersection of what you're good at, the environment you want to be in, the work that brings you joy and the service you offer others—you'll open up to fantastic possibilities. This is where you'll live your purpose and find the highest levels of achievement, success, and self-satisfaction.

Let's move on to the next section, which will give you a bird's-eye view of this model via ten key tips.

My Circle of Values

"Is that what they call a vocation, what you do with joy as if you had fire in your heart, the devil in your body?"
Josephine Baker

MY CAREER HEALTH

TEN TIPS

(This section provides a condensed summary of the first two Rebel Diva books. For details and worksheet guides, look at *Your Rebel Dreams* and *Your Rebel Plans*. Feel free to skip this section if you've already gone through the first two books.)

1. KNOW YOUR PURPOSE

Your personal values are the building blocks of your life and the framework by which you live.

They're your inner compass which guides you when life throws you curveballs. Learning about your values will teach you what you're made of and what your purpose in life is. Aligning everything you do with this purpose is what will create meaningful work, work where you'll thrive, not just survive.

But our purpose won't fulfill us if we use it for purely selfish means. Simon Sinek, author of the book *Start with Why: How Great Leaders Inspire Everyone to Take Action*, says, "Only when the pursuit to work to our full potential includes working to help others…do we actually find what we're looking for."

If we have a purpose in life that's larger than ourselves, our successes will be greater than we can imagine.

So, before anything else, identify your values, discover your purpose and think how it could uplift yourself as well as those around you.

2. LIVE FOR YOUR OBITUARY

We can live either for our obituary or our resume, but creating a life that's worth talking about after our death is much more worthwhile and more fun than any swanky CV. As legendary businessman Warren Buffett said, "Taking jobs to build up your resume is the same as saving up sex for old age."

To throw another metaphor into this heap, make sure you're not scaling a mountain you didn't want to climb in the first place.

To do this, you must determine what you're good at and what work brings you joy. Reflect on what impact you want to have on the world and what value you can offer others.

It's when we find answers to these questions, we'll discover passion work that will give us a fulfilled life.

The lucky among us know these answers from a young age. Others find their passions at thirty, forty, fifty and some even at eighty. Martha Stewart didn't start her business till her late forties, and Colonel Sanders opened his first Kentucky Fried Chicken shop at the age of sixty-four. It's never too late to uncover our passions.

So, how would you like to live your life? For your resume or your obituary?

3. EXPLORE YOUR PASSIONS

If you feel stuck or unsure of where your passions lie, it's probably because you haven't experienced the many diversities of life yet.

If you're young and confused about what you're supposed to do "when you grow up," this is the best time to experiment to your heart's content. Now is the time to travel, try your hand at different jobs, meet as many people as you can, and ask all the questions you have without fear of looking silly or being rejected.

If you're older but still feel stuck, have you explored all your talents? Have you worked in one career all your life? Have you attempted to learn new skills and attempt new things? Are you ready to take risks and go beyond your comfort zone? If not, the time to start is now.

We all have a general idea of what we like to do and what we don't like. It's when we attempt a variety of pursuits that we stumble on what we love to do. These are the activities that will put us in a state of flow, where time goes by without us noticing.

Don't be afraid to check out all the areas you're interested in until one of them leads to what you enjoy doing above all else. This will be what calls out to you. You'll know in your heart that you want to follow it with all you've got.

Take a crack at several ideas before you settle on one path.

4. SET YOUR GOALS

As author and thought leader Napoleon Hill said, "A goal is a dream with a deadline."

Finding your passion or having a wish in your head won't make it a reality.

Once you know what passions you want to pursue, the next step is to set solid goals to make them come alive. Then, write them down. Study after study has shown that people with written goals are fifty percent more likely to achieve them than those without.

One way to articulate your goals is using the SMART methodology. Make each of your goals Specific, Measurable, Actionable, Rewarding and Time bound.

And remember, while you must be hell-bent about your life dreams and vision, you can be flexible in how you reach your goals. You don't have to work on all your goals in one shot. You can phase each goal and work on a portion each time.

Whatever you do, don't stop at the dreaming and wishful thinking stage. Set SMART goals to create that life of passion you thirst for.

5. MAKE A PLAN

After you set your goals, a proper plan will help you identify a clear path to get to them.

Start by chunking your goals into bite-sized pieces. Then, reflect on the specific actions needed to complete each portion of your plan. Add a timeline, people to contact, places to go to, and the final results for each goal.

A plan doesn't have to be complicated. You don't need anything more sophisticated than a piece of paper and a pencil to make one. Keep it simple and easy to follow so you don't overwhelm yourself. Make sure you write it all down and review it regularly.

Remember, a plan is just that—a plan. Adjust it depending on circumstances or if your needs and wishes change.

Think of your plan as a treasure map that gives you the step-by-step guide to take you from where you are today to your future dream life.

6. TAKE ACTION

Your goals and your plan are of no use if you don't take the most important step of them all—action.

As motivational leader Tony Robbins likes to say, nothing happens without massive action. Once you do the thinking and the planning and the writing it all down, you must get out there and do the work.

The main barrier some create for themselves at this stage is to strive for perfection. If you wait to develop the most pristine plan or if you wait for everything and everyone to line up perfectly, you'll never start.

You must start even if you don't have all the information or resources at hand. Begin even if your plan isn't fully complete or you feel like you're not ready to start.

If you start, despite any miscalculations or failures, you'll still be ahead of the person who never began at all. While they're fiddling with the minutiae of their next steps, you'll have moved forward, tried something and learned a few lessons along the way.

The best way to start anything is to take the smallest step you can possibly take.

That first act will be the hardest, I can guarantee you that, but if you can overcome that, you'll do well.

Your first step will compel you to take the next one, and the next, and before long, you'll be completing your plans and achieving your goals, and well on your way to your dream life.

7. TRACK YOUR PROGRESS

The military has a saying that no plan survives contact with the enemy.

This doesn't mean the military never plans. In fact, this is one sector that plans extremely well, perhaps better than any other industry on Earth. They do so because they understand the power of a plan but are wise enough to know it needs to be tracked and adjusted as circumstances change.

Plans aren't carved in stone. They are powerful and essential maps that take us from A to Z, but the route can change. We may hit barriers or find shorter paths to the top.

So, stay vigilant, set regular checkpoints and make sure you're on track. Adapt your route to reflect your new reality and be okay with that.

Regular checks on our plan are crucial so we don't go astray or start climbing the wrong mountain and get lost.

Set a few goalposts to remind yourself when to review your progress and update your plan when needed.

8. ALWAYS BE LEARNING

To create the life where you do work you enjoy, you must cultivate a growth mindset.

This means you know that you don't know. In other words, you are aware there is always more to learn and that your capacity for knowledge and personal growth is limitless.

To increase your knowledge, you could read books, watch videos, listen to podcasts, talk to mentors, take classes, go to conferences and seminars, and listen to your role models speak, and never be afraid to ask questions. Talking to people or teams you usually don't hang out with can give you different perspectives and expand your knowledge in areas you may never have thought of otherwise.

Be the person who loves to explore many avenues and ideas and is innovative in how you solve problems. This will make your life more interesting and your work more enjoyable. This will also make others look at you as an expert in the field.

Always stay curious and always be learning.

9. THINK LONG-TERM

We're fortunate to live much longer lives than ever before.

Compared to our ancestors from the Middle Ages who ordinarily died at the grand age of forty, we now have twice as many years in our lives. We have better health care, improved understanding of nutrition and hygiene, and know more about mental and physical fitness, which have all translated into a higher quality of life and more of it.

We can undertake several careers in our lifetime. We have more opportunities to explore what we enjoy doing, and we may be able to transform several of our hobbies into a living. Whether we're twenty-five or fifty-five, we still have time to embrace a new career.

To do this, we'll need to try new things, adopt a sense of curiosity, and be brave enough to reinvent ourselves.

Journey through life with your eyes wide open. Explore new paths and ask yourself, *Who knows where this will take me next?*

10. MAKE YOUR CHOICE

Some cultures around the world still believe that a person's destiny has been chosen, even before birth. This belief is especially prevalent (and extreme) in traditional societies where there is little opportunity for personal growth and individual freedom.

This disturbing ideology is brought up whenever a young girl is carted off to undergo genital mutilation to suppress her sexual freedom or when she's bartered off to become a child bride to a man three or four times her age. Those who impose this violence wax lyrical about "a girl's destiny." They refer to the "will of god" or other such justification for inflicting this horror.

They do so because it's an efficient way to suppress resistance. The young child fears for her safety but she's now thinking, "What can I do? This is my destiny after all. This is the way it has been for my mother and my grandmother, and this is the way it will be for me."

Predestination is a brilliant tool to control others. Having someone believe in a fate enforced by a higher power serves an authoritarian's purpose well. So I'm not a fan of the word "destiny."

I am a strong believer in the unlimited capacity of human beings to make intelligent decisions and move in the direction we want, if we choose to do so.

This does not mean a young girl being assaulted by her forty-year-old "husband" somewhere in a Middle Eastern or North African village has a choice. No. The message here is the rest of us can create an environment that holds this truth to power so little girls like that won't be subject to brutality.

When we take ownership for our lives we not only catapult toward our own success but we become role models to young women everywhere as well. And this is not an impossible task. I know women in countries where they have few rights who've overcome unimaginable adversities to turn their lives around. I know women who had been forced into subjugation but fearlessly turned around to come out victorious. These brave hearts defied their "destinies."

If they can do it, we can too.

So if your parents or neighbors or society are telling you there's only one path to take and that your life is predetermined, they're only parroting what they've heard or what their own limited beliefs tell them.

In our modern world, we have options. We can put aside the masks society thrusts on us and dig deep within to find the secrets of our own desires. We can make the right choices and take action toward our dreams, regardless of what others say we must do.

If you live in a free society where there's ample freedom of expression, movement, and education, you have no excuse. Don't allow the misguided thought of predestination to sneak into your mind.

You must believe your future is in your own hands and that you can create your own destiny.

Give yourself permission to dream up your future. Dream big. Then dream bigger, darling.

THE HABIT MAKER

Let's Make These Stick

Pick one idea from the tips list and try it out for one month. Do this for thirty days and see how you do. Then, if you can, try a new one next month.

So, what is *one* action you'll take to incorporate career growth into your life this month?

Go back to the annual goal you set at the start of this section and make sure the activity you choose links to your goals.

Set January Activity:
Track the Activity: Check back at the end of the month to see how well you did
○ Great! I was Super Woman at this.
○ Good. I managed this most of the time.
○ Okay, I guess. I know I can get better.
○ Not so well. So, maybe I need to try this again. Who said you have to get it right the first time.
How can I improve next month?

Set February Activity:

Track the Activity: Check back at the end of the month to see how well you did

- ○ Great! I was Super Woman at this.
- ○ Good. I managed this most of the time.
- ○ Okay, I guess. I know I can get better.
- ○ Not so well. So, maybe I need to try this again. Who said you have to get it right the first time.

How can I improve next month?

Set March Activity:

Track the Activity: Check back at the end of the month to see how well you did

- ○ Great! I was Super Woman at this.
- ○ Good. I managed this most of the time.
- ○ Okay, I guess. I know I can get better.
- ○ Not so well. So, maybe I need to try this again. Who said you have to get it right the first time.

How can I improve next month?

Set April Activity:

Track the Activity: Check back at the end of the month to see how well you did

- ○ Great! I was Super Woman at this.
- ○ Good. I managed this most of the time.
- ○ Okay, I guess. I know I can get better.
- ○ Not so well. So, maybe I need to try this again. Who said you have to get it right the first time.

How can I improve next month?

Set May Activity:

Track the Activity: Check back at the end of the month to see how well you did

- ○ Great! I was Super Woman at this.
- ○ Good. I managed this most of the time.
- ○ Okay, I guess. I know I can get better.
- ○ Not so well. So, maybe I need to try this again. Who said you have to get it right the first time.

How can I improve next month?

Set June Activity:

Track the Activity: Check back at the end of the month to see how well you did

- ◯ Great! I was Super Woman at this.
- ◯ Good. I managed this most of the time.
- ◯ Okay, I guess. I know I can get better.
- ◯ Not so well. So, maybe I need to try this again. Who said you have to get it right the first time.

How can I improve next month?

Set July Activity:

Track the Activity: Check back at the end of the month to see how well you did

- ◯ Great! I was Super Woman at this.
- ◯ Good. I managed this most of the time.
- ◯ Okay, I guess. I know I can get better.
- ◯ Not so well. So, maybe I need to try this again. Who said you have to get it right the first time.

How can I improve next month?

Set August Activity:

Track the Activity: Check back at the end of the month to see how well you did

- ○ Great! I was Super Woman at this.
- ○ Good. I managed this most of the time.
- ○ Okay, I guess. I know I can get better.
- ○ Not so well. So, maybe I need to try this again. Who said you have to get it right the first time.

How can I improve next month?

Set September Activity:

Track the Activity: Check back at the end of the month to see how well you did

- ○ Great! I was Super Woman at this.
- ○ Good. I managed this most of the time.
- ○ Okay, I guess. I know I can get better.
- ○ Not so well. So, maybe I need to try this again. Who said you have to get it right the first time.

How can I improve next month?

Set October Activity:

Track the Activity: Check back at the end of the month to see how well you did
○ Great! I was Super Woman at this. ○ Good. I managed this most of the time. ○ Okay, I guess. I know I can get better. ○ Not so well. So, maybe I need to try this again. Who said you have to get it right the first time.
How can I improve next month?

Set November Activity:

Track the Activity: Check back at the end of the month to see how well you did
○ Great! I was Super Woman at this. ○ Good. I managed this most of the time. ○ Okay, I guess. I know I can get better. ○ Not so well. So, maybe I need to try this again. Who said you have to get it right the first time.
How can I improve next month?

Set December Activity:

Track the Activity: Check back at the end of the month to see how well you did
○ Great! I was Super Woman at this. ○ Good. I managed this most of the time. ○ Okay, I guess. I know I can get better. ○ Not so well. So, maybe I need to try this again. Who said you have to get it right the first time.
How can I improve next month?

SO, HOW DO YOU FEEL?

That's the end of this section. What do you think of the answers you gave here? If something wasn't captured in this section but you want to get it out of your system, this is the place to do so.

_____

_____

_____

_____

_____

_____

_____

_____

_____

_____

Tikiri

SECTION SEVEN

INVEST WELL

Wealth Health

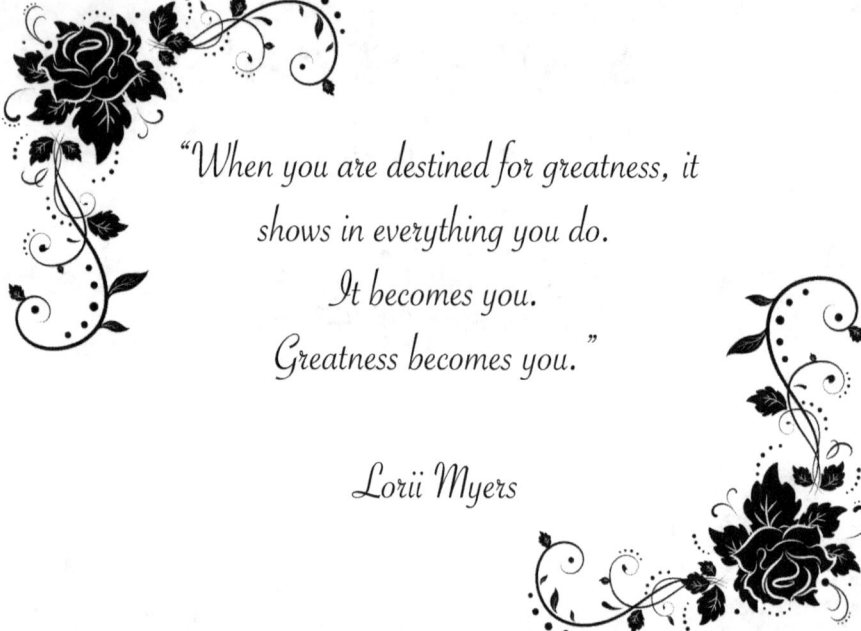

"When you are destined for greatness, it shows in everything you do. It becomes you. Greatness becomes you."

Lorii Myers

"The way to wealth is as plain as the way to market. It depends chiefly on two words, industry and frugality: that is, waste neither time nor money, but make the best use of both. Without industry and frugality nothing will do, and with them everything."
Benjamin Franklin

INVEST WELL

Our Financial Health

WHAT I'VE LEARNED ABOUT INVESTING WELL

We learn about almost everything in school, from calculus to sex education, yet we never get a primer on the one thing that occupies us for most of our adult lives—money.

This taboo of not talking about this pervasive instrument of our modern society harms us more than helps us.

OUR HISTORY

And women have it the worst.

In the generations before us, most women had little choice but to leave money management in their husbands' hands. In those days, men more commonly worked outside the home and earned an income. This is a generalization, of course. I know inspiring women who became professionals and successful businesswomen in previous eras, but they were a minority.

According to a recent study by the Retirement Income Literacy Gender Difference Report, over eighty percent of elderly women failed a quiz that asked basic questions on retirement planning, long-term savings, and investing. That eighty percent of our mothers and grandmothers are financially illiterate is distressing.

I now live in a part of the world where the largest and fastest-growing demographic is the gray-haired crowd. My colleagues in the financial sector tell horror stories of older women left in a lurch because they failed to keep an eye on their money, and even if they had wanted to, hadn't known where to begin. These women found themselves in dire straits when their spouses died or divorced them, forcing them to work at an age when most retire.

Women from cultures and families where they're treated as second-class citizens have it much worse. They're forced to rely on husbands, fathers, brothers, or other male "guardians" and have little independence to speak of—financial or otherwise.

So what about those of us who are fortunate to grow up in modern times and live in free societies?

OUR FINANCIAL AFFAIRS

Everyone reading this has pursued at least a basic education and most of us work for pay. We have more opportunities today than ever before to learn new skills, find a job, start a business, and make money. We now mostly work out of financial necessity, but it gives us a sense of independence and self-sufficiency.

So we should all be superwomen at managing money, correct?

Unfortunately, many women (and men) have no clue exactly how much they earn, owe, or require for their future. They live month to month, making impulse purchases, craving instant gratification, and consuming more than they earn. They use high-interest loans to buy everything from couches to cars, pay minimum levels on credit cards, and most times don't even look at their bank statements.

They balk at making a budget and continue living above their means, pretending everything will sort itself out one day. They have handcuffed themselves to a lifestyle they hate, but one they must now tolerate to justify their bad financial habits.

MATH CAN BE EASY

I blame this partly on the ridiculous tale we're fed as kids—that math is hard.

This despicable message was propagated further by the toys we were given as little girls. We learned from a young age to stick to inanimate objects that at most blinked their eyes and wore pink frocks, while our brothers and male cousins got mechanical gadgets and building blocks that trained and challenged their brains. This does not apply to all of us, but this is true for most girls.

The boy's games forced them to take risks, tackle problems, solve puzzles, and learn to fail. They didn't just play with toys, they created them, and in the process expanded their ability to think and calculate. Boys were never told, "math is hard."

The media, magazines, and television are no help. The programs they put on and the advertising they show reinforce these ludicrous stereotypes. No wonder none of my girlfriends want to draft a budget. Not everyone conforms to this view, of course, but I'm talking about the majority here.

We can't solve this problem using the popular and not-so-secret "Secret." Having a positive mindset or hoping for things to get better are fine, but we can't wish a debt away. Neither can we wish our rent or mortgage payments to reality.

What we must do is steel our stomachs and open our eyes wide. Take a hard look at your finances and ask the tough questions. Then, make the calculations and decisions to free yourself from your money troubles—not for one today or a weekend, but for a lifetime.

Financial illiteracy is not an issue only affiliated with older populations or in places where women are suppressed by tradition. It's a problem we all face. The good news is we can do something about it.

LET'S BECOME INVESTORS

We must not only get our books in order but also learn to invest.

We shouldn't just strive to have enough money to buy our favorite makeup kit or that dream car, but to *own* parts (or wholes!) of the very companies that create and sell these products to us. Why the heck not? *Investing* should be our ultimate financial goal.

There's so much to financial literacy than what I can share in this brief section. The topic of investing is beyond this introductory workbook, but you can read ten basic tips to increase your financial IQ here. Hope they help. Good luck.

THE STATE OF MY WEALTH HEALTH TODAY

First, four key stock-taking questions.

1. How are you doing in this pillar of your life right now?
○ Great! I'm Super Woman at this. ○ Okay. I know things can be better but it's not too bad. ○ Not too well. I wish things were different. ○ Meh. I'm not at all interested in this area.

2. Why is this area of your life important to you right now?

3. Who around you will get inspired when you start taking care of this part of your life?

4. What is your one main goal for enhancing your wealth health this year? We'll talk about specific tips and actions you can take on the next page, but for now, set an overarching goal for this area of your life for this year.

"You must gain control over your money or the lack of it will forever control you."
Dave Ramsey

MY FINANCIAL HEALTH

TEN TIPS

1. USE MONEY AS A TOOL

There's no intrinsic value in the dollar bill itself. Money is a tool to which we've given an agreed upon value.

We can use it for necessities like food and rent or to enjoy books, movies, and trips. We may need it to pursue an education or find better health care for the family. They say money makes the world go round, but it's only a means to pursue the important things in life.

We now live in an era of electronic banking that occur at lightning speeds across the globe. The revolution of blockchain technologies, bitcoin being one example, shows how even traditional currencies can change. The tool itself is improving, but it's still a tool.

But I often hear people say money is a dirty word. They believe anyone who seeks wealth has low values. I say, this is a defeatist notion based on false assumptions.

Money is not only a tool, but it's also a magnifier of one's principles and values.

If you're a good person and gain immense wealth, your kindness gets amplified proportionately. In the same vein, if you're a person with few scruples and get rich, your bad behavior is magnified, and you can now harm even more people. Given our negativity bias, it's these stories of evildoers we see and hear in the news that get entrenched in our memories. So we think money is bad and that anyone seeking it is unscrupulous.

What if we turn this around?

What if we compassionate and principled women and men get access to more resources? What if all the good people in the world stop thinking money is dirty and create wealth in legitimate ways and use it to service others? Their goodness will be intensified, uplifting everyone.

The main reason we don't see this often is because most of us good people sit back and play small. By doing so, we give space for the bad guys to do what they wish. Our apathy does nothing to serve the world.

It's time to stop fearing money. We must smarten up and make money work for us and everyone around us.

2. ARM YOURSELF WITH KNOWLEDGE

Knowledge is power. When you walk up to anyone armed with information, it's rare they'll attempt to lie or cheat because they know you *know*.

I've been educating myself on money and the markets since my early twenties. I read everything I could get my hands on about saving and investing. I took finance courses whenever I had extra electives in college even if it meant my tuition went up that semester. I was investing in knowledge.

Once I started working and had secured a small piggy bank of savings through frugal living, I decided to put my knowledge to the test. Instead of splurging it on a weeklong trip to a tropical resort, which was what my friends were urging me to do, I wanted to open an investment account.

I put my best dress on and walked up to my neighborhood bank to learn how this could be done.

After a few meetings, I realized I knew more about the basic principles of investing than them—those sharp-suited advisers sitting behind gleaming mahogany desks. I soon figured out their job was to hustle whatever investment packages the bank had already created, all of which had exorbitant management fees. They were mostly glorified salespersons.

I spent more than a month going around town talking to every bank, partly to educate myself and partly to find someone willing to answer my questions. What I finally concluded was no one would manage my money the way I would.

This is not to suggest you ignore the professionals and go for it on your own.

If you detest looking at your bills and statements, or if you don't have a clue about your current financial state, you will need help. Be careful how you select the experts though, as their incentives may be tied to increasing commissions for their employer and themselves than giving you the best advice you need.

If anyone refers you to a broker or adviser, don't be shy to ask how they're compensated and if they have additional incentives you need to know about. Most of them will be happy to share this information or tell you before you even ask. If they don't or if they hem and haw, run like mad in the opposite direction.

Educate yourself. Because knowledge trumps everything.

3. SET GOALS AND PLAN AHEAD

One of the best decisions I made after college was to set up financial goals—however meager those were at the beginning.

I now set aside one snowy January afternoon every year to write down my annual financial objectives. I identify the milestones I need to hit and the specific actions I need to take toward those goals.

Then, I slot these actions into my calendar so they stare me in the face every morning when I open my schedule. This forces me to take the actions I've planned for that day, that week or that month.

My initial focus was to repay the hefty student loan and credit card debt I'd racked up in college. Part of my motivation for creating a financial plan was the worry I'd not be able to repay it all and go bankrupt. It was a horrifying prospect.

I started my young adult life as an immigrant to the country with a few pennies in my pocket. I cleaned toilets to pay for rent and dug into the sale bins at the Salvation Army to find clothes for job interviews. At the time of my graduation, I had no one to turn to or a couch to crash on, so my eternal fear was ending up homeless. I had recurring nightmares of sleeping on a street corner, with a grimy blanket to keep me warm.

It was this scared little voice in my head and that homelessness image that got me on track. Funny, isn't it? It's when you are most vulnerable that you learn the most important lessons in life.

I've continued this planning habit for two decades now. This annual goal-setting, planning, and financial tracking allowed me to pay off all my debts. It also helped me to eventually buy my first car and condo with cash, years later.

So, set annual financial goals. If you stick to them and keep working at it, you'll make your dreams come true, whether it's a child's education, a new vehicle, a home, an exotic vacation, or early retirement. Yes, it's up-front work, but it will pay dividends for a lifetime.

4. AUTOMATE WHAT YOU CAN

Financial automation, in my opinion, is the best thing since the sliced bread.

I've automated recurring activities in my bank account ever since I figured out how. Soon after I started my first "real" job, I automated paying $250 of debt and putting away $50 in a savings account every month. As my income increased, I topped up these amounts.

If I had to stop, think and then make a decision about my savings and debt every time, I might have shrugged it off. I might have spent those funds on a fancy restaurant meal or two or splurged it to buy drinks for friends every night. But since these transactions happened immediately and automatically, I cut my debt to zero within two years, and on a small income at that.

You may get your employer to set up automated deductions from your paycheck if they offer that service. Or you can do this yourself online.

Move five to ten percent of your monthly paycheck into a high-interest savings account or use it to pay off a debt. Make sure this is done automatically as soon as you get paid so you don't even know it's happening in the background. The nice thing about this process is your savings will get compounded over time, so you'll end up with more than you put in—and that's an even better feeling than discovering a five-dollar bill under your couch.

Sometimes you've got to trick yourself into doing the right thing.

5. MAKE A BUDGET

Having a budget means being aware of how much is coming in and how much going out every month. It also means tailoring your lifestyle to what you have, not what you wish you could have.

In January of every year, I create a budget based on my annual goals. I put down my monthly expenses on a spreadsheet and break it into groceries, utilities, education, gas, health insurance, car maintenance, and even entertainment and travel if I can afford it that year.

Once you do this, you'll be amazed at how little you need to live on. You'll also see how much of your monthly expenses can be used for big decisions like paying down debt or saving up for an exotic trip. You'll become more conscious of how you spend, and you'll stop making frivolous purchases almost automatically.

Your first step is to create a budget. Your next is to track it.

Looking at your numbers every month will open your eyes. You'll see areas you can cut back on and you may even find areas with a surplus (this is an amazing feeling!). Use the information to make adjustments to your spending and savings throughout the year.

When you use a budget, you'll be forced to face your finances head-on rather than bury your head in the sand and hope things will work out eventually. Take thirty minutes once a month to go over your finances. Make sure to involve your spouse and family.

I may be more anally retentive than most (okay, I may be an extreme case of anal retentiveness), but I'm a firm believer that planning and tracking your money are two good paths to financial independence.

6. BE A SMART SHOPPER

Buying consumer goods with money we don't have is a terrible idea. I'm sorry if it hurts to hear this, but this is an important tip.

Whenever you get the impulse to shop using debt, here are a few basic questions to ask yourself: *Is this something I really need, or is this a nice-to-have? If I buy this, what other things will I have to scale back on?* And finally, *Do I really need this loan and why can't I pay for this in cash?* If the answers to all three questions put a knot in your stomach, walk away. Fast.

If you need a new sofa but don't have the cash to buy the fancy three-seater leather recliner in the window, ask yourself if you can make do with something different. Go to a consignment store where they have interesting and gently used items, or go online and comparison shop, and negotiate prices if possible.

The smartest way to buy anything consumable—goods that depreciate as soon as you buy them like clothes, electronics, furniture, and even cars—is to save up and pay cash.

If you have no choice but to get a consumer loan or buy something on lease, first ask for a better rate. The worst thing that can happen is they say no, but you'll have shown that you won't roll over and take everything at face value. They'll respect you for it and might even give you other incentives to keep your business.

Second, do some quick math to find out how much you'll be paying in total. When you see advertisements for car loans, they never tell you the full story. They happily share your monthly payments, but you need to step back and ask what you'll be paying in full at the end.

When you look at the numbers from twenty feet away, you may be surprised to learn you'll be paying twice, three times or even more than if you paid in cash. Advertisers and dealerships capitalize on staying silent on this little extra calculation.

Always do the math, ask all the questions to get the full picture, and negotiate wherever you can.

7. KNOW BAD DEBT FROM GOOD

Not all loans are the same. Some are good while some are bad for you. Knowing the difference can help you create a sound financial foundation that doesn't give you the sweats at three in the morning.
So what's good debt?

If you take out a loan to create something of value you can use in the long-term, that's good debt. This includes student loans for a trade program or a university degree, both of which increase your skills and may even give work experience in your field. These programs are designed to increase your future income, so using debt to purchase them can be a smart thing, as long as you don't abuse it.

Good debt can also be a loan to start a business that will give you future profits, or investment capital to grow your business.

Nothing is guaranteed but these activities can increase your income and improve your standard of living in the long run. Good debt means investing in your future.

What's bad debt then?

If you lease a luxury Corvette you can't afford, buy the latest trendy lamp or sofa on a loan, or go on an expensive trip to Hawaii with borrowed money, you might find yourself neck deep in bad debt soon. None of these decisions provide long-lasting value or increased income in the future. The Corvette will give you hours of untold fun, but sadly, you can't bank that fun and it will only last till your money runs out anyway.

Another bad debt is remortgaging your home or getting a home equity loan to buy a stock that your uncle Benny recommended at the weekend barbecue. Impulse decisions like this can heighten your financial problems rapidly, especially if you find you can't pay the loans back on time (yes, even to Uncle Benny). You could lose your biggest asset, which for many of us is our home, and that's a surefire way to get trapped in a financial black hole for years.

It's important to understand the quality of the debt you seek. Good debt can be harnessed to create a better future for yourself. Bad debt should never be accessed.

8. KNOW THE HIERARCHY OF DEBT

If you already have several loans and feel saddled with debt, there are a few key steps to get yourself out of that hole.

There was a time in my life, soon after college, when I was floundering in credit card debt plus huge student loans. I couldn't see how to pay back any of it in the foreseeable future. A scared little voice at the back of my mind kept reminding me how close to homelessness I was. So I went into overdrive to get my finances settled.

I looked at all my loans and calculated how much I owed. I prioritized my debt according to total principal and interest rates. Then, I decided to pay off the highest interest loans as quickly as possible.

Once I had this information figured out, I called each of the lenders and asked for a reprieve. I expected them to hang up on me. Not only did they stay on the phone, they, to my surprise, brainstormed solutions with me. A few places even offered to reduce interest rates after just one phone call. That was when I realized all I needed was to plan ahead and ask politely.

Six months later, I took it a step further. I called those same credit card lenders again. I explained my full debt picture and asked if they'd be willing to combine all my credit card bills, even those from other financial institutions. My goal was to get a better rate with one company. Again, I was surprised no one hung up on me. I consolidated all my credit card debt with one firm that gave me a rate as low as what I was paying for my student loans. That felt good.

But I didn't stop there.

I took on two jobs to increase my income, automated my debt payments, and continued to live frugally. My goal was to pay back all my debt come hell or high water. I finally paid back every penny in less than two years after graduation. That was $45,000 done, and I still can't believe I did that. I'm sharing this to say if I could do this, anyone can.

Look at your debt structure, figure out how much you're paying in interest, talk to your lenders and ask them to help you out. Once you have a strategy they and you agree with, stay focused on getting rid of that debt until it's down to zero. This is not the time to go on vacation, buy that expensive outfit or try the new restaurant in town. It's time to buckle down and do what you must do for the sake of your future.

Once you've paid all your debts, and if you continue with the same level of income, you'll be in the blissful position of having extra money to reward yourself—utterly guilt-free.

9. LIVE WITHIN YOUR MEANS

One of my principles is to always live below my means.

While in college, I lived in a small rented basement room in a university neighborhood. I shared a kitchen, a bathroom and a living room with four other students which kept my expenses low. When I graduated, I continued that student lifestyle until I paid back all my debt.

This wasn't my only option. Since I was finally making an income, I could have paid the minimum amounts on my loans and partied it up for a year or so. I could have dated several guys and eventually married one, having 2.5 kids, a dog and getting a huge house in the burbs—complete with car payments and a mortgage I'd be on the hook for a lifetime.

From observing older friends and from speaking in private with them, I realized that path could lead to getting stuck somewhere down the line. I'd be shackled to debt I couldn't pay off. I also knew it would be easier to keep my frugal way of living now than having to downsize under duress later on.

So, I found a small en suite room for rent close to work. I could walk to my new office and didn't have to worry about bus passes or car leases. I discovered a small group of like-minded friends and spent my free time on nature hikes, beach picnics, and neighborhood potlucks—all less costly than hanging out at nightclubs or expensive bars. Looking back now, it's these simple activities which cost nothing that were the most fun and memorable. This is how I paid back my debt so quickly.

Later in life, when I left my corporate job to become an entrepreneur, I used this same philosophy to take me through the initial rough start. Setting up a business is never easy and is wrought with risk. So, I cut back on my expenses and created a three-year financial plan that was much more frugal than what I was used to as a six-figure salaried employee.

Since I'd already learned to live within my means, this transition wasn't impossible. It felt like the most logical step to take. Sure, I worried and wrestled with self-doubt but financially, I could rest easy. I was grateful I didn't have to stay stuck in a job I no longer enjoyed and could finally follow my dreams.

Live within your means and you'll minimize your financial headaches. It will be freeing in ways you can't even imagine now.

10. DELAY GRATIFICATION

Have you heard of the famous marshmallow test?

Stanford University conducted a research study in the late 1960s and early 1970s to explore the impact of self-discipline on success. In this study, the researchers gave a group of children a marshmallow each and told them if they waited till they returned, they'd get two marshmallows. Shortly after, the scientists sneaked into an observation room and watched how the kids would react.

A majority of the children gobbled up their marshmallow as soon as the adult left the room. But, a few tried really hard not to eat their juicy sweet. They fiddled with their hair, sang to themselves, looked away at other objects in the room, and did their darnedest to not give in to temptation.

The study didn't stop there. They followed these children for decades afterward and discovered those who had summoned the willpower to wait for a second marshmallow were far more successful in all areas of life than those who didn't. This is a powerful story that shows the impact of self-control on success.

Why do almost seventy percent of lottery winners end up bankrupt? It's because they don't have the patience to use their windfall wisely or the know-how to plan. They spend and spend to impress themselves and those around them, and like the kids who ate their first marshmallow, wonder how it all disappeared so quickly.

If we can teach ourselves to become more conscientious in how we manage our money, we'll be well on our way to a successful life.

This doesn't mean living like a hermit in a secluded forest (unless you want to). We can start with the easy things. We can think twice about the cheap junk we buy impulsively.

We can begin by not reaching for the candy on the shelves near the cashier. We can then move on to more significant items like that car we buy to impress the neighbors or those crystal-studded, knee-high, three-inch patent leather boots (hey, I've had my moments of weakness too) we know we'll never wear.

Willpower is like a muscle and strengthens the more we work it. So, start small. And work your way up to paying off all your debt, increasing your savings and making investments that will keep you in good stead for life.

THE HABIT MAKER

Let's Make These Stick

Pick one idea from the tips list and try it out for one month. Do this for thirty days and see how you do. Then, if you can, try a new one next month.

So, what is *one* action you'll take to incorporate financial health into your life this month?

Go back to the annual goal you set at the start of this section and make sure the activity you choose links to your goals.

Set January Activity:
Track the Activity: Check back at the end of the month to see how well you did
○ Great! I was Super Woman at this. ○ Good. I managed this most of the time. ○ Okay, I guess. I know I can get better. ○ Not so well. So, maybe I need to try this again. Who said you have to get it right the first time.
How can I improve next month?

Set February Activity:
Track the Activity: Check back at the end of the month to see how well you did
○ Great! I was Super Woman at this. ○ Good. I managed this most of the time. ○ Okay, I guess. I know I can get better. ○ Not so well. So, maybe I need to try this again. Who said you have to get it right the first time.
How can I improve next month?

Set March Activity:
Track the Activity: Check back at the end of the month to see how well you did
○ Great! I was Super Woman at this. ○ Good. I managed this most of the time. ○ Okay, I guess. I know I can get better. ○ Not so well. So, maybe I need to try this again. Who said you have to get it right the first time.
How can I improve next month?

Set April Activity:

Track the Activity: Check back at the end of the month to see how well you did

- ○ Great! I was Super Woman at this.
- ○ Good. I managed this most of the time.
- ○ Okay, I guess. I know I can get better.
- ○ Not so well. So, maybe I need to try this again. Who said you have to get it right the first time.

How can I improve next month?

Set May Activity:

Track the Activity: Check back at the end of the month to see how well you did

- ○ Great! I was Super Woman at this.
- ○ Good. I managed this most of the time.
- ○ Okay, I guess. I know I can get better.
- ○ Not so well. So, maybe I need to try this again. Who said you have to get it right the first time.

How can I improve next month?

Set June Activity:
Track the Activity: Check back at the end of the month to see how well you did
○ Great! I was Super Woman at this. ○ Good. I managed this most of the time. ○ Okay, I guess. I know I can get better. ○ Not so well. So, maybe I need to try this again. Who said you have to get it right the first time.
How can I improve next month?

Set July Activity:
Track the Activity: Check back at the end of the month to see how well you did
○ Great! I was Super Woman at this. ○ Good. I managed this most of the time. ○ Okay, I guess. I know I can get better. ○ Not so well. So, maybe I need to try this again. Who said you have to get it right the first time.
How can I improve next month?

Set August Activity:

Track the Activity: Check back at the end of the month to see how well you did

- ○ Great! I was Super Woman at this.
- ○ Good. I managed this most of the time.
- ○ Okay, I guess. I know I can get better.
- ○ Not so well. So, maybe I need to try this again. Who said you have to get it right the first time.

How can I improve next month?

Set September Activity:

Track the Activity: Check back at the end of the month to see how well you did

- ○ Great! I was Super Woman at this.
- ○ Good. I managed this most of the time.
- ○ Okay, I guess. I know I can get better.
- ○ Not so well. So, maybe I need to try this again. Who said you have to get it right the first time.

How can I improve next month?

Set October Activity:
Track the Activity: Check back at the end of the month to see how well you did
○ Great! I was Super Woman at this. ○ Good. I managed this most of the time. ○ Okay, I guess. I know I can get better. ○ Not so well. So, maybe I need to try this again. Who said you have to get it right the first time.
How can I improve next month?

Set November Activity:
Track the Activity: Check back at the end of the month to see how well you did
○ Great! I was Super Woman at this. ○ Good. I managed this most of the time. ○ Okay, I guess. I know I can get better. ○ Not so well. So, maybe I need to try this again. Who said you have to get it right the first time.
How can I improve next month?

Set December Activity:
Track the Activity: Check back at the end of the month to see how well you did
○ Great! I was Super Woman at this. ○ Good. I managed this most of the time. ○ Okay, I guess. I know I can get better. ○ Not so well. So, maybe I need to try this again. Who said you have to get it right the first time.
How can I improve next month?

SO, HOW DO YOU FEEL?

That's the end of this section. What do you think of the answers you gave here? If something wasn't captured in this section but you want to get it out of your system, this is the place to do so.

Your Rebel Life

SECTION EIGHT
THINK WELL

Mental Health

> "It took me quite a long time to develop a voice, and now that I have it, I am not going to be silent."
>
> Madeleine Albright

"I am not afraid of storms for I am learning how to sail my ship."
Amy March

THINK WELL

Our Mental Health

WHAT I'VE LEARNED ABOUT THINKING WELL

When our psychological and emotional well-being is at its peak, it stimulates our capacity to think, expands our creativity, and makes us better learners. A healthy mind solves problems faster and heightens our productivity. The quality of our engagement with others improves, enabling us to forge stronger and more meaningful relationships.

But our mental health doesn't exist in a vacuum. It's closely related to our physical well-being.

When we dwell on negative thoughts, that invariably impacts our bodies. If not managed well, those thoughts and subsequent feelings can manifest as a sickness. When we're subject to long-term mental stress and unhappiness, our immune system gets compromised and we can become susceptible to even chronic illnesses.

Our minds and bodies are inextricably linked. Taking care of one means taking care of the other.

A SPECTRUM OF EMOTIONS

Let's remove one misconception right now. Being mentally healthy doesn't mean we'll find ourselves in a permanently happy mood.

Sadness, shame, grief, hurt, anger, tension, and disappointment are all part of life and can come to us at any time. It's impossible to go through several days continually feeling positive—at least not for us mortal, thinking, feeling beings who experience the full spectrum of emotions.

When we're mentally strong, however, we're better equipped to cope with the negative feelings when they do arise.

Without that level of mental resilience, we're more likely to act out on those emotions on bad days. Or on the other extreme, we may ignore or repress them. We'll pretend they're not happening even though our mood and productivity say otherwise. Or we may suppress negative feelings with unproductive distractions or harmful addictions.

Mental stamina enhances our capacity to handle problematic situations and dilemmas in life. It reduces the risk of us falling into a state of inaction or depression. We become capable of managing ruminations of our past, anxieties of our future, and other mental storms we can get entangled during dark times.

MENTAL RESILIENCE

How do we become more resilient then?

One of the most effective ways I've learned to manage my negative emotions is to accept that state of mind and let myself sit in the feeling for a short while. This means allowing the emotion to pass through me without acting on it immediately.

As I sit with it, I ask myself why I feel the way I do, what triggered it, and what I can learn from it. When I do this that feeling slowly flitters away. It's almost like a carrier pigeon with a letter in its mouth with an important message for me. Once I take the letter and read it, the bird's job is done, and it flies back to wherever it came from.

The length of time a negative feeling stays with us depends on the severity of the event that triggered it, but with this simple practice, I've found the time I dwell on a bad experience gets drastically reduced.

Allow your emotions to flow through you, especially those negative ones, while telling yourself, "I feel this way because that happened. I know where it's coming from, and that's okay. I'm only human." You may need to give it time, but soon, it too will pass, like anything else in life.

If you do this over time, you'll find you can better manage negative people, environments and events. You'll respond wisely rather than with knee-jerk reactions.

MANAGING OUR MINDS

Our minds may seem like esoteric things, something out of our control. But this is far from the truth. We can manage our minds, at least to some extent, if we only allow ourselves to.

Just like we must exercise our bodies frequently to stay fit, we also need to exercise our minds to protect their good health. Just like we have to schedule time in the week for a regular workout regime, we need to do the same for workouts of the mind.

In the next few pages, you'll find ten tips you can incorporate into your life as part of a healthy mental exercise regimen.

Choose one for a month, stick to it using the habit triggers and incentives mentioned earlier, and see how it goes. Then, the next month, check out another habit and ingrain that into your lifestyle.

Little by little, you'll enhance your mental stamina and you'll feel stronger. This will be useful on those days when things go awry and you need to rustle up the courage to tackle life's challenges.

Warning: Some of us may suffer from chronic mental problems which require medical treatment. The tips in this section aren't meant to alleviate suicidal thoughts, post-traumatic stress disorder, or any serious symptoms.

If you're in a constantly agitated state that seems unmanageable, please visit your physician and talk to them about it.

At the very least, speak with a friend and let them know the trauma you're going through so they may support you. You're a precious human being and you deserve to live a healthy, happy, distress-free life. Take care of yourself.

THE STATE OF MY MENTAL HEALTH TODAY

First, four key stock-taking questions.

1. How are you doing in this pillar of your life right now?

- ○ Great! I'm Super Woman at this.
- ○ Okay. I know things can be better but it's not too bad.
- ○ Not too well. I wish things were different.
- ○ Meh. I'm not at all interested in this area.

2. Why is this area of your life important to you right now?

3. Who around you will get inspired when you start taking care of this part of your life?

4. What is your one main goal for enhancing your mental health this year?

We'll talk about specific tips and actions you can take on the next page, but for now, set an overarching goal for this area of your life for this year.

"If you get the inside right, the outside will fall into place."
Eckhart Tolle

MY MENTAL HEALTH

TEN TIPS

1. LEARN TO MEDITATE

Among many other health benefits, meditation helps us stay calm and focused, especially during chaotic times. It increases self-awareness and teaches us how to become more mindful.

If you're new to meditation, here are a few tips on how to start. There are several techniques you can use, but focusing on your breath is the easiest to learn.

First, find a quiet place where you won't be disturbed. You don't need more than five minutes to begin. You can fit this in even between meetings or calls.

Sit in a comfortable position in a chair or on the floor and close your eyes. Now breathe in and out as usual, but become more conscious of it. Feel your breath coming in and out of your body.

While you're breathing mindfully, thoughts will flit in and out of your head. Some will sneak in quietly, and others will reel in like a full-blown movie with a soundtrack.

The best way to manage these thoughts is to first accept them by saying to yourself, "That's a thought." Then say, "You can go now." Don't judge the thought or yourself. Don't force yourself to stop thinking. This simple exercise is about becoming aware of what's going on inside your mind. Nothing else.

If you find it hard to let go of thoughts, try this meditation exercise used by the US Navy SEALS in their training program. I found this works best on days when I'm not settled or I'm too frazzled to meditate.

I sit cross-legged in a quiet and comfortable spot and take a few deep breaths in and out. After five normal breaths, I count silently from one to five as I slowly breathe in. When my lungs are full of fresh air, I hold my breath for a count from one to five. Then, I slowly let out my breath as I count again to five. Finally, I hold for another five counts while my lungs are completely empty. Then, I repeat the process.

The last step is the most challenging as your brain will start to panic, thinking it's out of air, though you know very well it's for a short duration. These five seconds will hone your focus. You'll find you don't have space for extraneous thoughts other than those about your breath. This will train your brain to concentrate.

If you do this for five to ten minutes every day, you'll eventually become more aware of what's whirring inside your head as you go through your day. This is a first and powerful step to enhancing your mental fortitude.

2. SHOW GRATITUDE

At one point in my childhood, I lived in a remote village in Asia where the night light came from kerosene lamps and the toilet was a tiny outhouse.

We had no plumbing, so my little sister and I had to walk to a well to bathe. Every week, we'd spend hours washing our clothes at that well and drying them outside. Though this was decades ago, I still marvel that I can get hot and cold water easily by opening a tap. I think it's wonderful that light comes on with a flick of a switch. My clothes washer and dryer are my best friends because I know how much time and energy they free up for me.

While this might sound a little strange to many of you, these feelings of gratitude for banal everyday things make me content, even happy.

Psychologists say gratitude is one of the healthiest emotions we can show. It's impossible to feel grateful and hold a negative thought in your mind simultaneously. Try it.

The easiest way to manage a negative feeling is to think about what you're thankful for at that moment. This is a surefire way to boost your mood.

I also keep a journal on my bedside table, and every night write down the one thing I feel most grateful for that day (other than running water and home appliances!). This two-minute activity has helped me get a better night's rest because the last thought in my head before I go to sleep is a positive one. This practice has also helped me become more mindful throughout the day.

I wasn't always like this. When I worked at my corporate job, I was the most irritable person I knew. I forgot about the hardships of my childhood, and I didn't have an ounce of gratitude in me. I'd get frustrated at every little thing and most days, I'd walk under a dark gray cloud. It was after several weeks of practicing gratitude that the dark cloud dissipated and I began to invite more sunshine into my life.

After that, I started actively seeking things to be grateful for, which reduced my negative temperament and gave me a happier outlook on life.

I now revel in things as simple as a sunrise. I'm grateful I'm alive to see this natural phenomenon every morning. It reminds me of the elegance of nature and how lucky I am to witness it from my bedroom window. The level of joy in my life has increased exponentially with these simple daily gratitude practices.

3. KNOW YOUR CIRCLE OF CONTROL

Trying to take charge of things you can't control can be like beating your head against a concrete wall studded with nails. You're hurting yourself badly and getting zero results. Focusing on what you can control will give you much greater peace of mind and stop you from wasting precious energy.

I learned this the hard way.

Remember when one of the largest recorded tsunamis hit Asia and Africa on Boxing Day in 2004? Hundreds of thousands of lives were lost, millions left homeless and entire regions devastated. As soon as I heard this news, I took out all the money I had in my savings account—money I'd saved for decades to buy my first home—and donated it all to a large well-known international aid organization.

Imagine my searing anger when a few years later, news reports came out saying most of the donations that went from that organization to my birth country had been siphoned off by corrupt government officials and terrorist groups who sold, yes, sold the food and supplies to the very people who needed them.

My blood pressure rises just thinking about that right now. I was ashamed to see such disgraceful behavior from my own motherland. I was furious at the ineptness of that aid organization and vowed to never donate again.

It took months for me to calm down and come to terms with it. I finally realized that I had given with the best of intentions and after that, it had all been out of my control. My anger would result in nothing except a future heart attack. So I had to let go.

I took control over what I could do and that was to promise myself that from then on, I'd do more research and give to smaller, more transparent groups led by caring individuals on the ground, doing the hard work. And to also never trust the administration of a country that sits high on the global corruption index.

The first step to understanding your circle of control is to delineate between what's internal and what's external to it. Examples of what's within your circle of control are your thoughts and actions. Outside of this are what others think and say and do.

Your circle of control is not a static picture and can change depending on your life experiences, circumstances, access to resources and ability to influence others. Take a snapshot of what this picture looks like for you today. Acknowledge your current state of affairs and consciously let go of the need to rein in things outside your circle of control.

This mindset shift can remove headaches, reduce anxieties, and allow you to focus on what you can improve. This, interestingly, expands your circle of control because you're reaching your goals and enhancing your capacities.

4. STOP BLAMING

The minute we stop blaming others for our problems is the minute we take control of our future. A mentally strong person takes responsibility for their actions, and don't blame their past, their background, or their environment.

Perhaps someone's words or actions hurt you in the past, but ruminating on those events will take you further down the rabbit hole of unhappiness. When we dwell on what someone did to us, we prolong our pain. It's like we're carrying them on our shoulders, giving them permission to continue antagonizing us.

Someone once said harboring resentment is like allowing the perpetrator to live rent-free in your mind. Do you really want to allow that?

Forgiving is not the same as forgetting. You can forgive for your own sake, but that does not mean what the other person did was right. It means you've regained control over your mind.

Learning from past encounters so you can avoid them in the future is a great first step. Learning to let go and move on is a second great step to enhance your peace of mind and gain mental strength.

5. DON'T SWEAT IT

None of us goes through life unscathed. One way to make things easier for us is to distinguish between significant problems and insignificant ones.

At face value, this is an easy problem to solve, but what I've found is we often react to the loudest noise nearby, not paying attention to the impact it can have on us—the squeaky wheel syndrome.

Take a step back and ask how a situation or an event will affect you before you decide on an action. If the impact is negligible, let go without feeling guilty. The time you spend torturing yourselves about small problems or issues you have no control over is not worth it and will only hold you back from happiness and success.

So ignore those neighbors you rarely bump into but who get under your skin. Ignore those annoying colleagues with bad habits at the office. And especially ignore snippy comments on social media by anonymous trolls. Ask yourself if their problem is worth your time.

Then ask yourself how much this issue will matter to you six months from now. How about a year from now? By doing this, you'll preserve your energy to tackle the more important things in life, which is what you should focus on and what will get you ahead.

6. ALWAYS BE LEARNING

This is the third time you've come across this tip in this book. Yes, it's that important.

Learning can be fun, intellectually stimulating, and will keep your brain engaged and strong as you age. Having an inquiring mind can keep you feeling young and mentally healthy.

It's impossible to know everything in this universe of ours, so there's always an opportunity to master a new skill, learn a new language, or try a new experience, regardless of how many degrees you've amassed, books you've read or countries you've visited.

Stay curious, keep a list of new things you yearn to learn about and pursue them via books, videos, seminars, conferences, courses, mentors, or travel. The more active your brain, the healthier and younger you'll feel and look.

The section on Knowledge Health gives more tips on how to foster a learning and growth mindset. Go back and read it if you haven't yet.

7. TALK ABOUT IT

Keeping problems steaming in our heads is never helpful.

When we share our concerns with others, we unburden our hearts and open ourselves to new ideas and solutions we may not have thought of by ourselves.

No one is above seeking for or receiving advice. Asking for help doesn't mean we're weak. It's a sign of strength and intelligence that we can recognize our limitations and seek assistance.

Another good habit is to settle issues as quickly as we can. Whenever I keep a problem in my head for too long, it transforms into a monster I can no longer control. My frustration and anger grow with it and the problem blows up, unnecessarily so.

If you're having issues, especially with someone close to you, it's best for your sanity as well as theirs to broach the topic, as fast as possible. Do this respectfully and truthfully. Even if the other party fails to acknowledge their role in the problem or turns away and ignores you (in which case you may want to rethink the future of that relationship), you'll feel lighter for having tried to clear the air.

8. SET BOUNDARIES

Some of the biggest headaches in our lives come from saying yes to the wrong things with the wrong people.

If you allow it, there are many who will happily, mostly unwittingly, suck your time, energy and sense of peace. Be careful whom you say yes to. Give yourself a pat on the back every time you affirm your boundaries. This is not easy to do, especially with those close to you.

The first step to building mental stamina is to clearly establish where your boundaries lie. If you completed the values exercise in *Your Rebel Dreams*, the first book of this series, you'll have a strong understanding of your values and know exactly which lines people can and can't cross.

This is a powerful place to be, and not something a majority of people have mastered. When you do this, you gain credibility among your peers and friends. They may not like that they can't meddle with you any longer. But they'll respect you for it.

The second step to strengthening your mental muscle is to ask yourself honestly if you really want to do what's being proposed. The best advice I've heard is that if a request doesn't elicit a "hell yes!" from you then it's invariably a "hell no!"

Don't accept invitations to make someone else feel good. Trying to please others and fit into the in-crowd was what we did in high school. We're adults now. Such behavior will build resentment inside you over the long-term. Your true feelings will be hard to suppress, and your grudges will boil over in one way or another someday.

I recently made a promise to myself that I'd give out the nicest "no's" anyone gets. This applies whether it's a guy I'm not interested in asking me on a date or a friend asking me for donations for a cause not on my radar. I say "I'm flattered you asked, but my answer is no, I'm afraid. But thank you so much for reaching out," or something to that effect. I say this in a kind tone, with a friendly smile and making eye contact so they know I'm being direct and honest. I don't have to give an explanation to anyone unless they're very close to me.

I call this the sandwich approach where my "no" goes in between an acknowledgment and an appreciation. And it works every time. They never bother me with the question again but they respect me and want to stay friends.

So, be honest with yourself and others. Learn to say no firmly but politely. It's hard at first but gets easier every time.

9. FIND THE RIGHT TRIBE

Figure out what kind of people you want to be around. Then, find them and keep them close.

The folk you want to stay away from are those with values diametrically opposed to yours. Learn to spot them quickly and avoid them. Life's too short to spend with those who don't treat themselves or you right.

Find friends with values similar to yours. They may not look like you or sound like you or even come from the same background as you. It's their values and principles that matter, and how they treat others and themselves. Such people may be rare and hard to discover, so it may take time, but be patient.

Once you find this tribe of yours, nurture the relationships. Keep your circle small and tight and give them the encouragement, support, and love they seek. Think of them as your potential future pallbearers, or you theirs.

This holds especially true if you're seeking a partner or spouse. The single most important relationship you'll have in life, apart from the one you have with yourself, is with your intimate partner. Be discerning of whom you choose and take the time to make the right choice. Never let your family or community or others decide this for you. And, never, ever rush this important decision. Ever.

10. LEARN TO ADAPT

Obstacles in life are inevitable. If you train yourself to prepare for and adapt to whatever comes your way, you'll sustain a greater balance in your life and reduce stress.

This doesn't mean sitting passively, letting things happen to you. It means staying alert to your environment, being prepared for potential outcomes, and responding appropriately to events, depending on their significance.

Strive to see the many sides of a problem so you don't get tunnel vision. Be flexible in your responses and find creative solutions to recover faster.

But remember, we can't prepare for everything in life. Neither should we, because that would be a futile exercise which can freeze us into inaction or put us in a straight jacket. We need to consciously decide when and where we will hedge our bets for whatever action we're taking.

If you can cultivate a mindset that accepts uncertainty as part of life and be flexible in how you respond to problems, you'll skillfully maneuver your way through life's challenges.

The accompanying Rebel Diva booklet, *The Fear Buster*, shares three tools to assess future risks in life. There's a link at the back of this book where you can download that book for free.

THE HABIT MAKER

Let's Make These Stick

Pick one idea from the tips list and try it out for one month. Do this for thirty days and see how you do. Then, if you can, try a new one next month.

So, what is *one* action you'll take to incorporate mental fitness into your life this month?

Go back to the annual goal you set at the start of this section and make sure the activity you choose links to your goals.

Set January Activity:
Track the Activity: Check back at the end of the month to see how well you did
○ Great! I was Super Woman at this. ○ Good. I managed this most of the time. ○ Okay, I guess. I know I can get better. ○ Not so well. So, maybe I need to try this again. Who said you have to get it right the first time.
How can I improve next month?

Set February Activity:
Track the Activity: Check back at the end of the month to see how well you did
○ Great! I was Super Woman at this. ○ Good. I managed this most of the time. ○ Okay, I guess. I know I can get better. ○ Not so well. So, maybe I need to try this again. Who said you have to get it right the first time.
How can I improve next month?

Set March Activity:
Track the Activity: Check back at the end of the month to see how well you did
○ Great! I was Super Woman at this. ○ Good. I managed this most of the time. ○ Okay, I guess. I know I can get better. ○ Not so well. So, maybe I need to try this again. Who said you have to get it right the first time.
How can I improve next month?

Set April Activity:
Track the Activity: Check back at the end of the month to see how well you did
○ Great! I was Super Woman at this. ○ Good. I managed this most of the time. ○ Okay, I guess. I know I can get better. ○ Not so well. So, maybe I need to try this again. Who said you have to get it right the first time.
How can I improve next month?

Set May Activity:
Track the Activity: Check back at the end of the month to see how well you did
○ Great! I was Super Woman at this. ○ Good. I managed this most of the time. ○ Okay, I guess. I know I can get better. ○ Not so well. So, maybe I need to try this again. Who said you have to get it right the first time.
How can I improve next month?

Set June Activity:

Track the Activity: Check back at the end of the month to see how well you did

- ○ Great! I was Super Woman at this.
- ○ Good. I managed this most of the time.
- ○ Okay, I guess. I know I can get better.
- ○ Not so well. So, maybe I need to try this again. Who said you have to get it right the first time.

How can I improve next month?

Set July Activity:

Track the Activity: Check back at the end of the month to see how well you did

- ○ Great! I was Super Woman at this.
- ○ Good. I managed this most of the time.
- ○ Okay, I guess. I know I can get better.
- ○ Not so well. So, maybe I need to try this again. Who said you have to get it right the first time.

How can I improve next month?

Set August Activity:

Track the Activity: Check back at the end of the month to see how well you did

- ○ Great! I was Super Woman at this.
- ○ Good. I managed this most of the time.
- ○ Okay, I guess. I know I can get better.
- ○ Not so well. So, maybe I need to try this again. Who said you have to get it right the first time.

How can I improve next month?

Set September Activity:

Track the Activity: Check back at the end of the month to see how well you did

- ○ Great! I was Super Woman at this.
- ○ Good. I managed this most of the time.
- ○ Okay, I guess. I know I can get better.
- ○ Not so well. So, maybe I need to try this again. Who said you have to get it right the first time.

How can I improve next month?

Set October Activity:

Track the Activity: Check back at the end of the month to see how well you did

○ Great! I was Super Woman at this.

○ Good. I managed this most of the time.

○ Okay, I guess. I know I can get better.

○ Not so well. So, maybe I need to try this again. Who said you have to get it right the first time.

How can I improve next month?

Set November Activity:

Track the Activity: Check back at the end of the month to see how well you did

○ Great! I was Super Woman at this.

○ Good. I managed this most of the time.

○ Okay, I guess. I know I can get better.

○ Not so well. So, maybe I need to try this again. Who said you have to get it right the first time.

How can I improve next month?

Set December Activity:
Track the Activity: Check back at the end of the month to see how well you did
○ Great! I was Super Woman at this. ○ Good. I managed this most of the time. ○ Okay, I guess. I know I can get better. ○ Not so well. So, maybe I need to try this again. Who said you have to get it right the first time.
How can I improve next month?

SO, HOW DO YOU FEEL?

That's the end of this section. What do you think of the answers you gave here? If something wasn't captured in this section but you want to get it out of your system, this is the place to do so.

_____

_____

_____

_____

_____

_____

_____

_____

_____

_____

_____

Your Rebel Life

SECTION NINE
LOVE WELL

Relationship Health

"I can't think of any better representation of beauty than someone who is unafraid to be herself."

Emma Stone

"Do you want to meet the love of your life? Look in the mirror."
Byron Katie

LOVE WELL

Our Relationship Health

WHAT I'VE LEARNED ABOUT LOVING WELL

I'm a novelist who can happily spend days by myself plotting stories and creating characters, as long as I have dark Belgian chocolate and cups of Ceylon tea. But even I need to get out of my writing den occasionally to meet real flesh and blood people.

We're an interconnected species—one that relies on community and survives through contact with others.

This means the ability to choose the right people to surround yourself with and the capacity to sustain strong connections are invaluable skills. Being savvy in these areas will significantly impact your well-being and success in life.

So where do we start?

Paradoxically, the first step to building healthy friendships with others lies within us. The greatest relationship we can forge is the one we have with our own selves.

Just like we must put our oxygen mask on first before assisting others, we need to learn to care for ourselves before we can share those same good feelings with those around us.

As author and psychologist Jordan Peterson says, we have a moral obligation and an ethical responsibility to take care of ourselves. He says we make the world a worse place when we choose *not* to.

My simpler philosophy is this: If you can't love yourself, how can you love others?

LOVE AT HOME

I grew up in an environment where the word "love" was taboo.

Whenever I used it, the adults in my family cringed and admonished me for speaking of such trite things. The culture in which I lived as a child was more concerned about safeguarding rigid traditions even if they were harmful rather than showing any love, care or humility.

I'm sure some of you reading this have had similar experiences, especially if you grew up during a time or in a place where there was little respect for children and women.

Almost daily, I witnessed and experienced emotional whippings. I had a constant knot in my stomach, not knowing what nightmare the next day would bring. It was the adults in the family who either perpetrated the mental terror or turned away and shrugged their shoulders as if to say there was nothing they could do to stop it.

This didn't bring out the best in me. I became an unbearable child who hated herself and those around her and lashed out at everything and anyone because that was all I saw. It took me years to understand the lessons from my childhood.

The most important lesson I learned was when a person doesn't love themselves, they become blind to the suffering of others. No amount of me speaking out or standing up against the abuse worked because everyone around me was grappling with such low self-confidence and extreme insecurity, they couldn't see past their own misery.

When someone doesn't love themselves, it's easy to become self-absorbed, paranoid, and even narcissistic. They don't understand the harm they're inflicting on others, let alone on themselves. My confused and angry younger-self was a great example of this. So I can only empathize with those who pretended nothing was wrong to preserve their sanity. I can even empathize with the bullies.

LOVE IN THE WORKPLACE

I saw more evidence of this—though not as extreme—as I became a young adult and started working.

The bosses I hated working for masked their self-doubt with a facade of overconfidence. They strutted around talking over others, belligerently so. They mistrusted their employees and played nefarious mind games to control their teams. From their behavior, I learned that manipulation is the choice weapon of the weak. Regardless of how they behaved outwardly, I could see the insecurity in their eyes.

After a few stints in different places, I looked for mentors and bosses who demonstrated self-awareness and who spoke their minds honestly and with integrity. I sought hard to find colleagues who took care of themselves and who showed a more balanced outlook on life. These were the people who inspired and motivated their teams.

I say this to show that before anything, *anything*, we must learn to love ourselves.

First, take the time to understand yourself better—reflect on your flaws, vulnerabilities, virtues, and strengths. Then, show care for your physical, mental, spiritual and intellectual health, like you'd put on that airline oxygen mask first. When you become mindful of who you are and how you treat yourself, you'll become empathetic and compassionate toward others as well.

Self-awareness and self-love are the first steps to building strong and long-lasting healthy relationships. They make for pleasant and caring environments in our homes, our workplaces, our communities, and even the world.

Begin with the woman in the mirror first.

THE STATE OF MY RELATIONSHIP HEALTH TODAY

First, four key stock-taking questions.

1. How are you doing in this pillar of your life right now?

- ○ Great! I'm Super Woman at this.
- ○ Okay. I know things can be better but it's not too bad.
- ○ Not too well. I wish things were different.
- ○ Meh. I'm not at all interested in this area.

2. Why is this area of your life important to you right now?

3. Who around you will get inspired when you start taking care of this part of your life?

4. What is your one main goal for enhancing your relationship health this year?
We'll talk about specific tips and actions you can take on the next page, but for now, set an overarching goal for this area of your life for this year.

"You, yourself, as much as anybody in the entire universe deserve your love and affection."
The Buddha

MY RELATIONSHIP HEALTH

TEN TIPS

1. CHECK YOUR SELF-TALK

Take stock of your self-talk.

Listen to the tone you use on yourself and think if you'd ever speak like that to a friend, your spouse, or a child.

For decades, ever since I was young, I used to self-flagellate with the words, "You stupid bitch. You're nothing." I said this to myself whenever I made a mistake, which was often.

These are words I'd never use on anyone else. If anyone had dared use them on me as an adult, I'd have walked away to never talk to them again. But I'd welcomed this toxic language into the intimacy of my head—a legacy from my childhood. Can you imagine the impact they must have had on my self-esteem?

Since then, I've learned to say, "It's okay, sweetie, you made a mistake. Let's move on." Yes, it sounds a little weird to call yourself "sweetie" at first, but it's much more gentle and kind.

This small shift over time has improved my sense of self-worth and brought dignity to my life. These good sentiments now spill out of me, and I am more patient and compassionate with others around me.

Before this revelation, I wasn't the nicest person to be around. I was short on patience and even shorter with my temper. People irritated me, crowds annoyed me and I despaired to deal with maddening humans every day. Whenever I caught an error, I'd berate the person involved with no regard to their feelings.

I now reach out and say gently, "It's okay. This won't kill us. Let's move on, shall we?" And I move on.

Show love for yourself. When you do, you'll turn into the person everyone will enjoy being around.

2. BE SUPPORTIVE AND ENCOURAGING

When we're attempting something new or challenging, we yearn to hear encouraging words from those around us. When we're going through tough times, we need people close to us who can hold, hug, and support us. The best way to receive these positive intentions is to be generous with them first.

Reach out to your loved ones when they need a kind word. Cheer them on when they're engaged in an important or demanding task. In a healthy relationship, all parties are mindful of the other's state and emotions and nurture each other through life's trials.

Ironically, I've found it easier to find someone to listen when I'm in need, but harder to find someone to cheer me on when I'm undertaking difficult and new tasks. It took a while to understand why. I realized not everyone has the same level of aspirations as me, and if my dreams are bigger than what they can imagine, that can scare them off.

Friends and family might think your ideas are crazy and even shout you down. They may fear success will change you, so their insecurities bubble up and squash your enthusiasm. They may not even realize they're raining on your parade, but these kinds of responses can make you want to give up on your dream. So be careful with whom you share your vision.

Protect your dreams from anyone who may object simply because they can't see as far as you can.

One promise I've made is if anyone, *anyone*, comes with shining eyes and a bright idea, I'll always be the one to say, "Go for it! Life's too short not to follow your dreams." Because I know the unlimited potential for human capacity and ingenuity.

3. PROJECT POSITIVITY

Having grown up in an environment laced with anger and fear, I've always had a hard time trusting others.

I used to be suspicious of strangers and made quick judgments to minimize potential harm, but this also meant I kept attracting more negative people. For a long while it seemed every taxi driver, waiter and store cashier was rude, dismissive and condescending. As they say, you invite what you fear. So I kept meeting people I didn't want to get to know.

Then one day, I heard author Brendon Burchard, one of my virtual mentors, talk about projecting positivity by giving others the benefit of the doubt. A simple idea but extremely hard to practice.

After trying it out many times, cautiously at first, my interactions with strangers became much more pleasant. I noticed the cashiers at the store and the waiters at the restaurants had become warmer and friendlier. Not all, mind you, but given my mindset shift, I started to see more of them. And when I smiled, they smiled back.

If you're having the same trust issues as I had, perhaps projecting positivity might help you attract the right people to your life.

Now, there's no need to smile at the creepy man who's leering at you from the street corner. There are limits to everything including this sentiment. Stay smart and safe.

4. SET BOUNDARIES

Setting boundaries doesn't mean you're being unfriendly. It means you're wise enough to know your self-worth and have consciously decided who gets close to you, when, how, and how often.

Some of us, especially women, have a bad habit of giving away our power to everyone else. This happens when we've lost confidence and don't know where to draw the line, so we acquiesce to other people's demands, feeling terrible while doing so.

Once you've done some introspection, understand your fundamental values and learn to show self-care, your boundaries will become clear. You'll know exactly how you want others to treat you and interact with you. When you get to this point, the outside world will see your confidence, and this will make it harder for them to disrespect you.

This is a powerful place to be and one of the best ways to create healthy relationships.

Remember, no one can read your mind, nor you theirs. Discussing your needs openly and gently can help you create a positive environment that will strengthen your connections.

5. DEAL WITH CONFLICT

Conflict is a part of life. Unpleasant interactions can come from a random stranger cutting you off on the road, a colleague at work who's envious of your project or a spouse mad at you for leaving the dishes in the sink again. When this happens, I try not to overthink the event to the point of ruining my day. It's not worth it.

If they're strangers, I let it go. I don't know if they've had a bad day or something terrible is happening in their lives that's showing up in how they're presenting themselves. So I don't waste my energy trying to engage with them or convince them.

If the relationship is important, though, I do my best to manage the problem as soon as it comes up. This way, the incident is still fresh on everyone's minds, and I don't allow it to build into a huge and unwieldy octopus in my mind.

If you ignore conflicts and hold on to them for a long time, you'll build resentment which can manifest itself in ugly ways. Our bodies are good at absorbing repressed emotional energies, so resolving issues quickly can keep you healthy in mind, body, and in relationships.

I've noticed, time and time again, the unhealthiest families and some dysfunctional workplaces frequently have someone at the top who's afraid of conflict and shuns it like the plague. This makes disagreements fester until they smell bad, and even then, they might splash a bit of perfume and say everything is okay.

Sidestepping conflict is nothing to be proud about. It makes everyone around you uncomfortable and resentful, and it's hurtful to others. Plus, it never resolves the root cause of the matter. So, deal with conflict appropriately and promptly.

6. AGREE TO DISAGREE

It's impossible to find someone who agrees with you all the time. If they do, that would be somewhat weird and creepy, wouldn't it?

The people we need to seek aren't those who concur with everything we believe in, but are intelligent enough to know we can have different viewpoints and can agree to disagree in a reasonable and friendly manner.

A disagreement can be an opportunity to learn something new and grow closer to the other person, as long as all parties are open, honest, and share their ideas respectfully.

Choose your battles wisely, though.

If the other person is not someone you plan to continue a relationship with or is someone you prefer not to get close to, ask yourself if a conversation is worth your time. If not, don't spend your precious energy trying to have a debate. The wisest thing you can do is nod, smile, and walk away quickly.

This holds especially true for online trolls. Life's too short to entertain little people.

7. ASK FOR AND GIVE HELP

Most of us, and I count myself here, find it hard to ask for help. We'd rather not burden others with our problems, so we don't get help until it's too late.

A colleague once told me of a time when her husband had a heart attack in the middle of the night. He didn't want to wake her up because she had an important interview the next morning. So he dragged himself as quietly as he could to the guest bedroom and struggled with the pain until he realized the severity of the issue and called for help.

This example is perhaps drastic, but I think we all need to learn to ask for help at the right time from the right people and make space for others to ask us the same in return.

Being transparent and frank with our own struggles and showing our vulnerabilities usually creates a trusting environment that allows others to open up. This, in turn, builds stronger and more long-lasting bonds.

Don't be afraid to reach out. Our friends and family might even appreciate the gesture.

8. LEARN TO APOLOGIZE

We all make mistakes. We're only human.

If we can be honest with ourselves and those around us and offer our frank apologies where warranted, we'll increase trust exponentially.

We see this even in the cold world of business. Companies spend millions and decades building trust with their consumers to lose it all in a matter of seconds when they're discovered to be covering up a grievous error. It's those businesses that show immediate accountability for their mistakes and apologize who gain even greater customer loyalty.

People normally understand and forgive as long as it's not a heinous crime. For individual relationships, a simple apology is all that's needed.

So, stay sincere, be responsible, and take accountability for your actions. Apologize when you make a mistake, and move on. This will do wonders for how people will regard and respect you.

9. LEARN TO FORGIVE

Forgiveness doesn't mean forgetting.

It means you can remove that burden of hurt from your shoulders and put it down. Otherwise, it will sit heavy, cutting into your skin, hurting you even more and slowing you down.

As author Lewis Smedes said so beautifully, *"To forgive is to set a prisoner free and discover that the prisoner was you."* Forgiveness allows us to cut ties that hold us to our past and enables us to move into the future.

It doesn't matter if the person who did you harm acknowledges your forgiveness or even cares for it. Their crime will be a burden for them to bear for the rest of their lives, and karma will get them eventually. I'm sure of it.

I know this is so much easier said than done.

It took me decades before I could forgive people from my past. Even though no one has recognized my forgiveness and may never do so, I've moved on, knowing I'm no longer carrying toxic feelings of resentment inside me. This doesn't mean I condone that behavior or that I'll return to that environment of toxicity. While my mind is free, I'm clear where my boundaries lie.

Learn to forgive and then let go. Do it for your own sake.

10. LEARN TO LET GO

Not all relationships are meant to last forever.

Friendships can become stagnant and people can grow apart. The unhealthiest response you can make is to cling to connections that are no longer working. Letting go of friends, colleagues, or even family members who have outstayed their welcome, especially if they are harmful to you, is essential to a stress-free and healthy life.

When someone consistently brings you pain even after you've discussed it with them, it's time to reassess. Ask yourself where the relationship is heading and if it's beneficial to both of you to continue.

You have no obligation to endure the hardship of a bad relationship, no matter how close you are to that person. Doing so can trigger physical sickness, mental unrest, and heartache. As hard as it is, cutting such ties will be the best decision you'll make.

Listen to your instincts. Our bodies know how a relationship is affecting us well before our minds tell us. Be brave and never let others guilt-trip you for taking a step forward to a happier life. This will require courage, but nothing good comes without effort, and you'll be far better off afterward.

Best of all, letting go will create space for new people to come into your life—people more aligned with your values and principles.

CAUTION

If you're in a relationship with someone who harms you and your children verbally, emotionally or physically, please think twice about what you're fostering and teaching your young ones. No amount of trying to understand or coax the perpetrator will lead to a healthy environment. That would be the most noxious liaison you can have. And your children will pay dearly for it later on in life. I should know. I'm a product of such an environment.

Be wary of people who never reconcile their words with their actions. Be especially careful of those who always have a handy excuse for their poor behavior or who are constantly mired in dramas of their own making. There are times to cut loose and let toxic people go. This is one.

Please summon up the courage, find help, and get the hell out of there. It is the right thing to do. Your children will forever be grateful to you for it. And you will finally find peace.

THE HABIT MAKER

Let's Make These Stick

Pick one idea from the tips list and try it out for one month. Do this for thirty days and see how you do. Then, if you can, try a new one next month.

So, what is *one* action you'll take to incorporate relationship health into your life this month?

Go back to the annual goal you set at the start of this section and make sure the activity you choose links to your goals.

Set January Activity:
Track the Activity: Check back at the end of the month to see how well you did
○ Great! I was Super Woman at this.
○ Good. I managed this most of the time.
○ Okay, I guess. I know I can get better.
○ Not so well. So, maybe I need to try this again. Who said you have to get it right the first time.
How can I improve next month?

Set February Activity:
Track the Activity: Check back at the end of the month to see how well you did
○ Great! I was Super Woman at this. ○ Good. I managed this most of the time. ○ Okay, I guess. I know I can get better. ○ Not so well. So, maybe I need to try this again. Who said you have to get it right the first time.
How can I improve next month?

Set March Activity:
Track the Activity: Check back at the end of the month to see how well you did
○ Great! I was Super Woman at this. ○ Good. I managed this most of the time. ○ Okay, I guess. I know I can get better. ○ Not so well. So, maybe I need to try this again. Who said you have to get it right the first time.
How can I improve next month?

Set April Activity:

Track the Activity: Check back at the end of the month to see how well you did

- ○ Great! I was Super Woman at this.
- ○ Good. I managed this most of the time.
- ○ Okay, I guess. I know I can get better.
- ○ Not so well. So, maybe I need to try this again. Who said you have to get it right the first time.

How can I improve next month?

Set May Activity:

Track the Activity: Check back at the end of the month to see how well you did

- ○ Great! I was Super Woman at this.
- ○ Good. I managed this most of the time.
- ○ Okay, I guess. I know I can get better.
- ○ Not so well. So, maybe I need to try this again. Who said you have to get it right the first time.

How can I improve next month?

Set June Activity:

Track the Activity: Check back at the end of the month to see how well you did

- ○ Great! I was Super Woman at this.
- ○ Good. I managed this most of the time.
- ○ Okay, I guess. I know I can get better.
- ○ Not so well. So, maybe I need to try this again. Who said you have to get it right the first time.

How can I improve next month?

Set July Activity:

Track the Activity: Check back at the end of the month to see how well you did

- ○ Great! I was Super Woman at this.
- ○ Good. I managed this most of the time.
- ○ Okay, I guess. I know I can get better.
- ○ Not so well. So, maybe I need to try this again. Who said you have to get it right the first time.

How can I improve next month?

Set August Activity:

Track the Activity: Check back at the end of the month to see how well you did

- ○ Great! I was Super Woman at this.
- ○ Good. I managed this most of the time.
- ○ Okay, I guess. I know I can get better.
- ○ Not so well. So, maybe I need to try this again. Who said you have to get it right the first time.

How can I improve next month?

Set September Activity:

Track the Activity: Check back at the end of the month to see how well you did

- ○ Great! I was Super Woman at this.
- ○ Good. I managed this most of the time.
- ○ Okay, I guess. I know I can get better.
- ○ Not so well. So, maybe I need to try this again. Who said you have to get it right the first time.

How can I improve next month?

Set October Activity:

Track the Activity: Check back at the end of the month to see how well you did

- ○ Great! I was Super Woman at this.
- ○ Good. I managed this most of the time.
- ○ Okay, I guess. I know I can get better.
- ○ Not so well. So, maybe I need to try this again. Who said you have to get it right the first time.

How can I improve next month?

Set November Activity:

Track the Activity: Check back at the end of the month to see how well you did

- ○ Great! I was Super Woman at this.
- ○ Good. I managed this most of the time.
- ○ Okay, I guess. I know I can get better.
- ○ Not so well. So, maybe I need to try this again. Who said you have to get it right the first time.

How can I improve next month?

Set December Activity:
Track the Activity: Check back at the end of the month to see how well you did
○ Great! I was Super Woman at this. ○ Good. I managed this most of the time. ○ Okay, I guess. I know I can get better. ○ Not so well. So, maybe I need to try this again. Who said you have to get it right the first time.
How can I improve next month?

SO, HOW DO YOU FEEL?

That's the end of this section. What do you think of the answers you gave here? If something wasn't captured in this section but you want to get it out of your system, this is the place to do so.

_____
_____
_____
_____
_____
_____
_____
_____
_____
_____

Tikiri

Your Rebel Life

SECTION TEN

PLAY WELL

Spirit Health

"No matter what you look like or think you look like, you're special and loved and perfect just the way you are."

Ariel Winter

"We don't stop playing because we grow old; we grow old because we stop playing."
George Bernard Shaw

PLAY WELL

Our Spirit Health

WHAT I'VE LEARNED ABOUT PLAYING WELL

Have you recently tickled a friend, admired the sunset or watched a hummingbird hover over a flower? When was the last time you jumped into a puddle? Or put your tongue out to catch a snowflake?

It's these small things that make us smile, laugh and raise our spirits. Plus, they don't cost a dime. So why don't we do these things more often?

We're so preoccupied with the urgent drudgeries of our grown-up lives, we forget we have only one life to live. And a short one at that. That's sad because it's when we no longer enjoy the little things we let our spirits die.

I've heard many people say they can't do the things they used to because they're constrained now as adults.

They hold demanding jobs needed to pay off huge mortgages. They spend most of their time stuck in traffic or in dreary offices with colleagues they don't particularly like. They have kids, spouses or ex-spouses who take away their energy and time.

Even if they had the time and space, they're too embarrassed about what others might think if they let loose and have some fun.

If you're letting anyone or anything stop you from having a "life," ask yourself if that's just an excuse.

IT DOESN'T HAVE TO BE THIS WAY

It's time to follow your heart and discover joy.

This section is all about rediscovering rapture in life. The tips here are self-explanatory and not new.

The mistake some people make is to engage in these activities or even make them habits without first becoming self-aware, without understanding their values or knowing how to make thoughtful decisions.

If you adopt these as habits while in a state of confusion or not fully understanding yourself, they can become escape routes from reality. They become hedonistic excesses which will dig you into a hole.

This is the reason I left this chapter till the end.

I hope you'll enjoy these final tips. Now go an reignite your days, feel alive and find bliss in the small things again.

THE STATE OF MY SPIRIT HEALTH TODAY

First, four key stock-taking questions.

1. How are you doing in this pillar of your life right now?

- ○ Great! I'm Super Woman at this.
- ○ Okay. I know things can be better but it's not too bad.
- ○ Not too well. I wish things were different.
- ○ Meh. I'm not at all interested in this area.

2. Why is this area of your life important to you right now?

3. Who around you will get inspired when you start taking care of this part of your life?

4. What is your one main goal for enhancing your spirit health this year?

We'll talk about specific tips and actions you can take on the next page, but for now, set an overarching goal for this area of your life for this year.

"Play is the only way the highest intelligence of humankind can unfold."
Joseph Chilton Pearce

MY SPIRIT HEALTH

TEN TIPS

1. BE CHILDLIKE, NOT CHILDISH

What happens when you unleash a toddler in a garden? They'll scramble around in joy. They'll pluck a blade of grass, sniff a flower, poke the puppy, or stare in rapture at a sunbathing ladybug.

When we were young, we thought the world was a wondrous place. We touched, smelled, tasted, ran, fell, got up, and ran again, gleefully giggling to ourselves. We were explorers of places, people, and our own potential. Every single moment was an adventure.

Let's rediscover this childlike nature which lies buried deep inside us.

Relearn how to become playful. Try new things without being afraid to fail. Get amazed at what you observe and experience every day. Do your own thing and don't worry about what others say. Start a journey not fully knowing how it might pan out and be okay with that.

Think of life as a garden where you've been unleashed, and you'll find more joy in your days.

2. TRY SOMETHING NEW

Kick excitement into your life by doing something totally new.

There's a program for everything under the sun, from studying a new language to exploring the stars, driving race cars, painting with your dog, or learning to cook a great Italian meal (or Chinese or Nigerian or Indian…). You can take a seminar, go to a conference, watch videos, listen to podcasts, or attend a class. The only limitations are your imagination and your wallet.

You can acquire knowledge and enjoy new experiences without spending a penny. We have the world at our fingertips today. The possibilities are infinite. Once you think of all the new things you want to attempt and learn, you'll find life's way too short. Pick one new thing you'd like to explore every year and try that. Have fun with it.

A jolt of novelty can invigorate you. It will give you an opportunity to meet new people and spur ideas for work you're already doing.

3. APPRECIATE ART

At the height of the Second World War, Winston Churchill was asked if he'd cut the budget for arts and culture to funnel the funds into the war effort. He replied, "Then what are we fighting for?"

How true. What good is emerging victorious from battle when all you're left with is a hollowed-out society?

I believe art, not money, makes the world go around. Art helps us to conceptualize diverse and difficult topics and understand complex issues. Art is where we retreat to when we're disheartened or yearn for an escape.

How many times have you got immersed in a book, a movie, or a television show to get away from reality for a short while? Art can be therapy. Getting lost in a song, a painting, or a story can help us forget our troubles and find joy, even if for a short while.

So where can you find art?

There's no need to visit the Louvre to appreciate art. That would be nice but you have opportunities in your own backyard. Look around your neighborhood to find a gallery or museum. Follow a school theater group, attend a community concert or go to the library to find free books. Take yourself to the cinema and check a matinee if you're strapped for cash. Head to your local pub on days they have live music shows or keep an eye out for street artists working their magic.

Experiencing art will uplift your spirits on days you need that pick-me-up. So, go find art and enjoy human ingenuity for the amazing gift it is.

4. CREATE ART

Just like we get joy from appreciating art, we can also find pleasure by creating it.

Making art can free our minds and tickle areas of the brain we don't access frequently. It allows us to get in touch with our intuition. It helps us enter a meditative-like flow state where everything around us recedes and we can focus intently on the one thing we're creating. This can be cathartic and even help us identify solutions to problems we're struggling with.

Art is anything that's created with our imagination to stimulate a visceral reaction in ourselves or others. It can be a song, a melody, a painting, a photograph, a mosaic, a sculpture, a novel, a poem, a dress, a one-of-a-kind piece of furniture, a mural, or even a building—if you're so inclined and have the resources.

The trick is to have fun and appreciate whatever we create without judgment.

We all have a little Leonardo da Vinci inside us, waiting to be tapped into. We shouldn't expect Leonardo-like results from our first attempt though. Or even our second.

Now, get out and express yourself!

5. ENJOY THE PROCESS

Most of us lead hectic lives filled with deadlines and milestones and things that need to get done yesterday. How can we enjoy life in the middle of all the demands that get piled on us?

Here's how I learned my lesson. One Monday morning, I decided to work thirteen-hour days for a week to finish a novel. I stuck to my plan and sloughed through the work, only getting up to use the washroom or to grab a sandwich from the fridge. I love writing, but this felt like a chore. But I'd made a promise to myself, and I'd keep it no matter what.

Imagine my surprise on Thursday morning when I went over my work and saw poor quality writing. I wanted to quit and throw the book away. I'd forgotten my brain and body needed time to recuperate for best performance. I'd also forgotten to enjoy the process.

I no longer aspire to sit for hours on end and write like a maniac. I break my days into forty-five-minute chunks, with five to ten-minute breaks in between when I do something completely different. I stretch, do yoga, go for a walk around the block, or get out on my patio and breathe in the fresh air.

When I come back to my desk, I feel refreshed and eager to get back to work. That's when I get into the flow and enjoy the task, without worrying about deadlines or whether I'd hit a goal. That's also when I produce quality results.

Setting ambitious goals and following a plan are important. But if you don't enjoy the process, you'll feel like dropping out and never finishing what you started.

As Ralph Waldo Emerson once said, "Life is a journey, not a destination." Enjoy your trip.

6. CELEBRATE SUCCESS

When was the last time you celebrated a success?

Whenever you achieve a goal or reach a milestone, stop and say "good job," so your achievements can sink in. This will motivate you to go to the next level.

Without internalizing our successes, we put ourselves at risk of going mindlessly from accomplishment to accomplishment and burning out. We'll wonder why we're doing what we're doing. We'll ask what the point of it all is.

When you find yourself asking these questions, you're walking the defeatist path—not a good place to be. So, give yourself recognition and appreciation, and you'll continue to be excited to reach your next objectives.

Having said this, be strategic about how you compensate yourself. If you reward yourself willy-nilly, it will minimize the recognition and your achievements. Also, make sure the reward is worthwhile and doesn't distract you from the goal you're trying to achieve.

7. GIVE

Do you remember the last time you gave a gift for someone you cared for? Part of the adventure was anticipating how they'd receive it, wasn't it?

You may have conjured up images in your mind of them opening the package and seeing their face light up as they pulled out whatever it was you got them. Didn't those thoughts send jolts of happy energy through you?

Giving to others is a wonderful way to uplift our spirits. The act of giving has as many perks for the giver as for the receiver. Studies have shown that when you give, it inspires those around you to give too, triggering a virtuous cycle.

When you give, your body boosts hormones like dopamine, serotonin, and oxytocin, which have long-term health benefits. These hormones trigger positive emotions, reduce high blood pressure, and lower inflammation. They reduce our social fears, increase our ability to trust, and enhance our sense of empathy. How great is that?

So keep giving for your own happiness. Think beyond tangible gifts that cost money. Share a hug, a compliment, a smile, or a simple acknowledgment. They work in the same way. And if you can give expecting nothing in return, you'll truly find joy.

8. GET SOCIAL

We, humans, are social animals. We thrive in groups and tribes and like to find people who think and act like us. This makes us feel like we're not alone. We get that warm and fuzzy feeling inside like we're connected to something bigger than us.

When you need a boost of happiness, ask a friend out for a coffee or lunch or take them out for drinks. Chitchatting, hugging, laughing, and sharing a meal with people you care for can boost your happy hormones and leave you with a blissful glow inside.

A network of good friends whom you can reach out to when in need is a healthy thing to have. Find people with positive outlooks who genuinely care about you and want the best for you. If you don't have that small circle of good friends yet, don't wait till you're in dire straits. Seek them out now.

If you already have a lovely circle, give them all a hug and remind them how much you appreciate them being around.

9. FIND YOUR HAPPY DIVERSION

I don't have many keepsakes because I moved frequently. Every time I moved, I had to throw things out to keep my luggage light. But there was one thing I lugged around wherever I went, ever since I was a child and that was my box-of-past-lives. This box contains photos, diaries, letters, postcards, and souvenirs from my travels and childhood.

I can sift through that box of treasures for hours, recollecting the places I've been to and the people I've met. One memento in this box is an ankle-length Mauritian skirt I wore for an amateur school show. This eye-popping tropical skirt reminds me of the camaraderie I had with an international group of girlfriends and the fun island song we danced to. It's little things like these that make me smile and turn a gray day into a beautiful one.

Find a simple activity you can retreat to on a rainy Sunday afternoon when you're feeling a little blue.

Getting lost in social media, as interesting as it can be, is out. Social media, in all its variations, is designed to be addictive and can make you feel worse off than when you began. Plus, it's a stupendous waste of time.

Maybe you have a box-of-past-lives like mine which will make you feel whimsical. Perhaps it's a favorite book or a fun board game. Maybe it's meeting a good friend for a cup of tea. Whatever it is, find that simple diversion that lifts you up and makes you feel good on days you don't feel like yourself.

10. TRAVEL

Mark Twain once said you only regret the things you don't do. If you've ever dreamed of traveling, do so now.

If you have the time and money and you're an intrepid traveler, look far and experience new continents and cultures. Don't wait till you retire or win the lottery to start.

Save extra every month, look for special deals, or share costs with friends. Explore creative solutions like offering to write a blog or take videos for sponsorship from travel magazines. Volunteer for an international aid organization. Restore a sailboat and sail by yourself.

But you don't have to cross oceans to travel. You can be a tourist in your own backyard. Take a train or drive to a destination near your home where you can rejuvenate and return feeling like you've had a mini adventure.

Do what works for you and what you're comfortable with, but never leave travel to when you're too old to get up and get moving.

Get out there and experience the world!

THE HABIT MAKER

Let's Make These Stick

Pick one idea from the tips list and try it out for one month. Do this for thirty days and see how you do. Then, if you can, try a new one next month.

So, what is *one* action you'll take to incorporate more playfulness into your life this month?

Go back to the annual goal you set at the start of this section and make sure the activity you choose links to your goals.

Set January Activity:
Track the Activity: Check back at the end of the month to see how well you did
○ Great! I was Super Woman at this. ○ Good. I managed this most of the time. ○ Okay, I guess. I know I can get better. ○ Not so well. So, maybe I need to try this again. Who said you have to get it right the first time.
How can I improve next month?

Set February Activity:

Track the Activity: Check back at the end of the month to see how well you did
○ Great! I was Super Woman at this. ○ Good. I managed this most of the time. ○ Okay, I guess. I know I can get better. ○ Not so well. So, maybe I need to try this again. Who said you have to get it right the first time.
How can I improve next month?

Set March Activity:

Track the Activity: Check back at the end of the month to see how well you did
○ Great! I was Super Woman at this. ○ Good. I managed this most of the time. ○ Okay, I guess. I know I can get better. ○ Not so well. So, maybe I need to try this again. Who said you have to get it right the first time.
How can I improve next month?

Set April Activity:
Track the Activity: Check back at the end of the month to see how well you did
○ Great! I was Super Woman at this. ○ Good. I managed this most of the time. ○ Okay, I guess. I know I can get better. ○ Not so well. So, maybe I need to try this again. Who said you have to get it right the first time.
How can I improve next month?

Set May Activity:
Track the Activity: Check back at the end of the month to see how well you did
○ Great! I was Super Woman at this. ○ Good. I managed this most of the time. ○ Okay, I guess. I know I can get better. ○ Not so well. So, maybe I need to try this again. Who said you have to get it right the first time.
How can I improve next month?

Set June Activity:

Track the Activity: Check back at the end of the month to see how well you did
○ Great! I was Super Woman at this. ○ Good. I managed this most of the time. ○ Okay, I guess. I know I can get better. ○ Not so well. So, maybe I need to try this again. Who said you have to get it right the first time.
How can I improve next month?

Set July Activity:

Track the Activity: Check back at the end of the month to see how well you did
○ Great! I was Super Woman at this. ○ Good. I managed this most of the time. ○ Okay, I guess. I know I can get better. ○ Not so well. So, maybe I need to try this again. Who said you have to get it right the first time.
How can I improve next month?

Set August Activity:

Track the Activity: Check back at the end of the month to see how well you did

- ○ Great! I was Super Woman at this.
- ○ Good. I managed this most of the time.
- ○ Okay, I guess. I know I can get better.
- ○ Not so well. So, maybe I need to try this again. Who said you have to get it right the first time.

How can I improve next month?

Set September Activity:

Track the Activity: Check back at the end of the month to see how well you did

- ○ Great! I was Super Woman at this.
- ○ Good. I managed this most of the time.
- ○ Okay, I guess. I know I can get better.
- ○ Not so well. So, maybe I need to try this again. Who said you have to get it right the first time.

How can I improve next month?

Set October Activity:
Track the Activity: Check back at the end of the month to see how well you did
○ Great! I was Super Woman at this. ○ Good. I managed this most of the time. ○ Okay, I guess. I know I can get better. ○ Not so well. So, maybe I need to try this again. Who said you have to get it right the first time.
How can I improve next month?

Set November Activity:
Track the Activity: Check back at the end of the month to see how well you did
○ Great! I was Super Woman at this. ○ Good. I managed this most of the time. ○ Okay, I guess. I know I can get better. ○ Not so well. So, maybe I need to try this again. Who said you have to get it right the first time.
How can I improve next month?

Set December Activity:

Track the Activity: Check back at the end of the month to see how well you did
○ Great! I was Super Woman at this. ○ Good. I managed this most of the time. ○ Okay, I guess. I know I can get better. ○ Not so well. So, maybe I need to try this again. Who said you have to get it right the first time.
How can I improve next month?

SO, HOW DO YOU FEEL?

That's the end of this section. What do you think of the answers you gave here? If something wasn't captured in this section but you want to get it out of your system, this is the place to do so.

Your Rebel Life

SECTION ELEVEN
MY PLEDGE

"Don't limit yourself. Many people limit themselves to what they think they can do. You can go as far as your mind lets you. What you believe, remember, you can achieve."

Mary Kay Ash

MY PLEDGE

I pledge to create and cultivate good health in all areas of my life.

I will improve incrementally and know that change happens one step at a time.

I will stay consistent in my habits and track my progress.

Today, I pledge to take action to create a better life and a successful future for myself and my loved ones.

Signature	

Date	

Your Rebel Life

"I am a strong woman. I don't sit around feeling sorry for myself, nor let people mistreat me. I don't respond to people who dictate to me or try to bring me down. If I fall I will rise up even stronger because I am survivor and not a victim. I am in control of my life and there is nothing I can't achieve."
Unknown

FINAL QUESTIONS

Before you go, I have two last questions for you:

1. After going through the exercises here, what's your definition of success now?

2. Has this changed from the answer you gave at the beginning of this workbook? Why do you think that happened?

SO, HOW DO YOU FEEL?

How do you feel after completing this book? What do you think of the answers you gave here? Write down anything that wasn't captured in any of the chapters but that you want to get it out of your system.

_____

_____

_____

_____

_____

_____

_____

_____

_____

_____

"Just when the caterpillar thought the world was over, she became a butterfly."

English Proverb

THANK YOU!

Thank you for dedicating time for yourself and for coming on this journey to create an amazing, shiny new you. Keep this book somewhere you can see every day to keep the momentum going. Go over your answers every month to check your progress and plan for the next year.

SIGN UP TO GET YOUR EXCLUSIVE GIFT!

This Rebel Diva booklet comes with three essential decision-making tools to help you overcome any anxieties when faced with life's challenges. Click on the cover or go to the link below to get your free copy and also learn about exclusive and free training at the Rebel Diva Academy.

Bust Your Fears

https://www.rebeldivas.com/rebel-life-page/

Come on over and join other Rebel Divas in our private **Facebook Group: Rebel Divas** to share your thoughts and dreams, learn new tips and get inspired.

http://www.facebook.com/groups/RebelDivas

Your thoughts mean a lot to me and I'd love to hear your feedback. It's also how I'll be able to give you what you're looking for. If you'd like to leave an honest review of this book, please do so here:

http://books2read.com/YourRebelLife

FIFTY BOOKS YOU MAY ENJOY

Here's an eclectic list of books I've read recently. They've inspired me and made me realize I wasn't alone in my journey to create a happy, healthy and harmonious life.

The authors of these books are trailblazing entrepreneurs, superstar business leaders, and amazing motivational speakers. They are the modern-day rebels.

Many have overcome great adversity and none of them had the world handed to them. Each and every one of them has worked hard, ignored naysayers, persevered through failure, and followed their lifelong passions.

This list is ordered alphabetically.

- *Big Magic: Creative Living Beyond Fear,* Elizabeth Gilbert
- *Blink: The Power of Thinking Without Thinking,* Malcolm Gladwell
- *Born for This: How to Find the Work You Were Meant to Do,* Chris Guillebeau
- *Chicken Soup for the Soul,* Jack Canfield (Editor) and Mark Victor Hansen (Editor)
- *Don't Sweat the Small Stuff…and It's All Small Stuff: Simple Ways to Keep the Little Things from Taking Over Your Life,* Richard Carlson
- *F.U. Money: Make As Much Money As You Damn Well Want And Live Your Life As You Damn Well Please!,* Dan Lok
- *15 Secrets Successful People Know About Time Management,* Kevin Kruse
- *Footprints on the Moon,* Seth Godin
- *Getting Over Getting Mad: Positive Ways to Manage Anger in Your Most Important Relationships,* Judy Ford
- *Getting to Yes: Negotiating Agreement Without Giving In,* Roger Fisher and William Fry

- *High Performance Habits: How Extraordinary People Become That Way*, Brendon Burchard
- *How Not to Die: Discover the Foods Scientifically Proven to Prevent and Reverse Disease*, Dr. Michael Greger
- *How to Stop Worrying and Start Living: Time-Tested Methods for Conquering Worry*, Dale Carnegie
- *How to Win Friends and Influence People*, Dale Carnegie
- *Ignore Everybody: And Thirty-Nine Other Keys to Creativity*, Hugh MacLeod
- *Letter to My Daughter*, Maya Angelou
- *Man's Search for Meaning*, Viktor E. Frankl
- *Mind Power Into the 21st Century: Techniques to Harness the Astounding Powers of Thought*, John Kehoe
- *Mindfulness, Little Exercises for a Calmer Mind*, Gill Hasson
- *Nice Girls Don't Get the Corner Office: Unconscious Mistakes Women Make That Sabotage Their Careers*, Lois P. Frankel
- *Orbiting the Giant Hairball: A Corporate Fool's Guide to Surviving with Grace*, Gordon MacKenzie
- *Play Like a Man, Win Like a Woman: What Men Know About Success that Women Need to Learn*, Gail Evans
- *Rich Dad, Poor Dad*, Robert T. Kiyosaki
- *Six Steps to One Million: How to Achieve Your Financial Dreams*, Gordon Pape
- *Smart Women Finish Rich: 9 Steps to Achieving Financial Security and Funding Your Dreams*, David Bach
- *The Alchemist*, Paulo Coelho
- *The Art of Happiness*, Dalai Lama XIV, Howard C. Cutler
- *The Blue Day Book, A Lesson in Cheering Yourself Up*, Bradley Trevor Grieve
- *The Five People You Meet in Heaven*, Mitch Albom

- *The Four Agreements*, Don Miguel Ruiz
- *The 4-Hour Workweek*, Tim Ferriss
- *The Girls' Guide to Power and Success*, Susan Wilson Solovic
- *The Little Book of Thinking Big: Aim Higher and Go Further than You Ever Thought Possible*, Richard Newton
- *The Miracle Morning*, Hal Elrod
- *The Motivation Manifesto*, Brendon Burchard
- *The One Thing: The Surprisingly Simple Truth Behind Extraordinary Results*, Gary Keller
- *The Power of Now: A Guide to Spiritual Enlightenment*, Eckhart Tolle
- *The Secret*, Rhonda Byrne
- *The Seven Habits of Highly Effective People: Powerful Lessons in Personal Change*, Stephen R. Covey
- *The Sleep Revolution: Transforming Your Life, One Night at a Time*, Arianna Huffington
- *The Spark: Igniting the Creative Fire That Lives Within Us All*, Lyn Heward and John U. Bacon
- *The War of Art: Break Through the Blocks and Win Your Inner Creative Battles*, Steven Pressfield
- *The Wealthy Barber: The Common Sense Guide to Successful Financial Planning*, David Chilton
- *Thick Face, Black Heart: The Asian Path to Thriving, Winning & Succeeding*, Chin-Ning Chu
- *Think and Grow Rich*, Napoleon Hill
- *What Color Is Your Parachute? A Practical Manual for Job-Hunters and Career Changers*, Richard N. Bolles
- *Who Moved My Cheese?* Spencer Johnson and Kenneth H. Blanchard

🌿 *Women Who Think Too Much: How to Break Free of Overthinking and Reclaim Your Life*, Susan Nolen-Hoeksema

🌿 *You Are a Badass: How to Stop Doubting Your Greatness and Start Living an Awesome Life*, Jen Sincero

🌿 *Your One Word*, Evan Carmichael

Your Rebel Life

FIFTY VIRTUAL MENTORS I FOLLOW

Here's a list of fifty thought-leaders I follow via their books, articles, podcasts, videos, talks, and interviews.

These virtual mentors of mine have inspired, motivated, and encouraged me to the point I now consider them almost family. And like any family, I don't agree with everything they say, but most of the time I find myself happily nodding as I listen to their life-affirming messages.

All of them are active online and almost all have given TED Talks and many interviews, so it's easy to find their content online.

This list is ordered alphabetically.

- Adam Braun
- Arianna Huffington
- Barbara Corcoran
- Bill and Melinda Gates
- Brendon Burchard
- Brené Brown
- Chris Guillebeau
- Danica Patrick
- Danielle LaPorte
- Daymond John
- Ellen DeGeneres
- Elon Musk
- Eric Thomas
- Evan Carmichael
- Gabrielle Bernstein
- Gary Vaynerchuk
- Gloria Steinem

- Iyanla Vanzant
- J.K Rowling
- Jack Canfield
- Jack Ma
- Jason Silva
- Jeff Bezos
- Jessica Jackley
- John Assaraf
- Jordan Peterson
- Kris Carr
- Leila Janah
- Les Brown
- Lewis Howes
- Lisa Nichols
- Marianne Williamson
- Marie Forleo
- Marissa Mayer
- Mel Robbins
- Michelle Obama
- Oprah Winfrey
- Patrick Bet-David
- Prince Ea
- Richard Branson
- Richard Dawkins
- Robin Sharma
- Sara Blakely
- Seth Godin

- Sheryl Sandberg
- Simon Sinek
- Tim Ferris
- Tom Bilyeu
- Tony Robbins
- Warren Buffett

THE REBEL DIVA SERIES

www.RebelDivas.com

The Rebel Diva workbooks are practical guides to creating the life you dream about.

They share lessons from the best self-help and personal development resources available today and synthesize them into simple guided exercises that anyone can follow without drowning in detail.

These books don't just tell you what you need to do. They take you by the hand and show how to follow through.

The tools and techniques here are simple, but their reach is deep. They're designed to make you contemplate your past, present, and future, and make you a visionary for your own life.

All the answers are in you. All these workbooks do is extract them one gentle question at a time and make you write them down, so you can take the first step toward your future.

These books aren't for your bookshelf. They are to be marked up, highlighted, and dog-eared with your scribbling all over the pages. Keep them on your bedside table with a pen, so you can reach them whenever you need a jolt of inspiration or want to track your progress.

BOOK 1 - YOUR REBEL DREAMS

This book will show you how to discover your purpose and ultimate passions in life.

You'll find practical exercises to help you create a vision for your life that matches your personal values and your unique personality.

Once completed, check back with *Your Rebel Dreams* once a year. Make it the thing you do every December 31st, just before you head out to the New Year's Eve party.

Uncover the amazing gifts you have in life!

The main sections in this book are:

1. My Values
2. My Flair
3. My Zone
4. My Joy
5. My Service
6. My Vision

BOOK 2 – YOUR REBEL PLANS

This book will show you how to make your dreams come alive.

You'll go through a series of easy exercises to help you identify your core goals and create an action plan for your life.

You'll learn how to track your progress and celebrate your successes. At the end of this workbook, you'll have a treasure map to your life dreams—a map that will help you stay on your game, no matter what.

Once completed, check back with *Your Rebel Plans* every three months to see how you're progressing. And to find a good excuse to reward yourself! You only need to spend thirty minutes each time to make sure you're on track.

The main sections in this book are:

1. My Goals
2. My Plans
3. My Check-ins
4. My Schedule
5. My Year

BOOK 3 – YOUR REBEL LIFE

This book will show you how to live a harmonious, happy and healthy life every single day.

You'll get access to one hundred tips for the ten most important pillars of your life. You'll learn how to design an amazing lifestyle that's in tune with the fundamental values you identified in Your Rebel Dreams and the ambitions you wrote down in Your Rebel Plans.

This is a standalone guide and can be read anytime. Take a thirty-minute coffee break at the end of every month to take stock of where you are and apply one more tip to enhance your life.

The main sections in this book are:

Environment:
- 1. Feel Well - My Environment Health

Health:
- 2. Sleep Well - My Rejuvenation Health
- 3. Move Well - My Physical Health
- 4. Eat Well - My Nutrition Health

Vocation:
- 5. Learn Well - My Knowledge Health
- 6. Work Well - My Career Health
- 7. Invest Well - My Wealth Health

Spirit:
- 8. Think Well - My Mental Health
- 9. Love Well - My Relationship Health
- 10. Play Well - My Spirit Health

ABOUT THE AUTHOR

Tikiri holds a bachelor's degree in international business from North America and a master's degree in management from Europe. She has over fifteen years of experience managing large-scale projects and corporate risk management programs and has studied, worked and lived in several countries across four continents.

Tikiri is the award-winning author of several fiction and nonfiction books and through her writing, champions women's and girl's rights around the world.

Okay, enough of the formal stuff...

My expertise doesn't come from a postdoctoral psychology degree. Neither do I profess to be a self-help guru of any sort. I'm still a work in progress and try to learn something new every day.

I started small. Very small. I began my career trying to sell Kirby vacuum cleaners door-to-door (nope, I didn't sell even one) and graduated to cleaning toilets (made a lot more than my vacuum-selling stint). I did this to pay for rent, ramen noodles, and tuition.

Like everyone else, I've muddled my way through life. I've been a traveler and an immigrant. I've been poor and desperate. I've been bullied and afraid. I've been heartbroken and devastated. And I'm a foreigner everywhere I go. Through all this, I've also seized opportunities to learn as much as I can, push myself and figure out how people think, behave and grow.

The most important lesson I've learned is if you stand in your power no matter what's going around you or how others treat you, things work out. They always do.

I've used my personal experiences and what I've learned from others to write these books. The lessons in here are what helped me create the life I desired, so I wrote these books hoping they will help you too in some way. Even if one sentence spurs you forward, I will have done my job.

To say hello and connect, come on over to www.TikiriHerath.com

A FREE STORY

THE RED-HEELED REBELS NOVEL SERIES

This is a gripping, coming-of-age, global suspense thriller series with iron-willed heroines who fight villains and traditions that keep them down. If you like exotic locales, complex twists, and globe-trotting female leads, you'll love this story.

What readers are saying:

> "A wonderful story! I didn't want to leave the characters."

> "A real page-turner and international thriller. Reminds me of why I've always loved to read. Because I can visit worlds and places I wouldn't ordinarily get to see."

> "If you love adventure, strong female leads and cultural insights, this is the perfect book for you."

> "A heart-stopping adventure. I just couldn't put the book down till I finished reading it."

> "This is soul writing that needs to be read."

To claim the prequel story to this series for free, go to

www.RedHeeledRebels.com

STUDIES REFERRED TO IN THIS BOOK

World Health Organization, Physical inactivity a leading cause of disease and disability, warns WHO
http://www.who.int/mediacentre/news/releases/release23/en/

World Health Organization, Worldwide obesity
http://www.who.int/mediacentre/factsheets/fs311/en/

Motivation dimensions for running a marathon
https://www.sciencedirect.com/science/article/pii/S2095254615001003

Delay of Gratification
https://www.britannica.com/science/delay-of-gratification#ref1206154

Childhood Obesity
http://childhoodobesityfoundation.ca/what-is-childhood-obesity/statistics

Meat Consumption and Cancer Risk
http://www.pcrm.org/health/cancer-resources/diet-cancer/facts/meat-consumption-and-cancer-risk
https://www.cancer.org/latest-news/world-health-organization-says-processed-meat-causes-cancer.html

10 Reasons Why Sugar is Bad for You
https://www.healthline.com/nutrition/10-disturbing-reasons-why-sugar-is-bad#section10

Tikiri

Your Rebel Life

www.ingramcontent.com/pod-product-compliance
Lightning Source LLC
Chambersburg PA
CBHW071951070526
44583CB00015B/1153